ISBN#0-931697-59-X

Published by
Casey Treat Ministries
P. O. Box 98800
Seattle, WA 98198

I Love This Thing Called Parenting...

Well, Most of the Time!

By
Wendy Treat

DEDICATION

To my cool kids: Caleb, Tasha, and Micah.
One of the greatest joys in my life is being your mom.
You three are completely unique, once in awhile
frustrating, but always totally amazing gifts from God!
Thanks for giving me the grace to make mistakes, the
respect to try it again, and the love that covers
everything else. Love you much!

CONTENTS

INTRODUCTION

My family always called me "the little mom." I was just eleven years old when our parents gave my siblings and me a darling baby sister from Korea. I used to call her "a little pumpkin," and I carried her around a lot. It has always been a big part of my personality to try to take care of everybody, making sure everyone was okay, and everything was in order. It is who I have always been, and obviously something God put within me from the youngest age.

When my husband, Casey, and I were first married everyone expected us to have children immediately. People were amazed when we didn't. The truth is that Casey and I were reluctant to have children because we saw so many of the great people in the Christian world whose children didn't grow up to love God. They were raised in the Church, but ran from everything to do with church and God the minute they were able. Many were involved with drugs and alcohol. I know that people can certainly overcome drugs and alcohol, but when a person who has been raised in the Church hates God and church, that's another problem altogether. Knowing we would be pastoring a church and raising our children in the Church concerned us. We wondered, *could we really parent our children properly?*

It was vital to Casey and me if we did have children, that they would grow up loving God. We knew we could handle all the other issues that come from being parents, but to live our lives to help people know God and love Him, yet have our own children turn away from Him would be devastating to us.

One day, after many years of marriage, I was at home praying. I had spent several hours in prayer because I felt like there was something missing in my life. I felt like I needed to connect with God in some way. At the end of this time of prayer I said, "Okay, God, am I missing something? Am I not doing something that I am supposed to be doing? Father God, I need some direction." As I took the time to be quiet and listen in my spirit, I heard Him simply say, "Children."

I was so excited. I thought, *do I really get to have them?* Casey and I had been married for six years at this point, and we had talked back and forth several times about the probability of raising godly children in today's world. We hadn't felt settled that it was the right time to start our family.

That afternoon when Casey came home, he ran up the stairs and came into our front room where I had been praying. As he sat down, I sat across from him and said, "I have something I want to talk to you about." He said, "Okay." I told him, "I want to have children," and he immediately said, "Me too!"

As we continued talking Casey asked me, "What happened?" (When he had walked in the door, he sensed that something was different.) I explained, "As I was praying God really showed me that we have to have children by faith, and we have to raise them by faith." Hebrews 11:6 says: *But without faith it is impossible to please Him...*

My mind had been consumed with fear and worry. I had based my thinking on my own ability, wisdom, and insight. I wasn't basing it on God's ability and the wisdom I found in His Word. I was trying to see how I could have children and raise them in my own ability.

What a wonderful journey and high calling it is to be a parent. It is a job fulfilled by courageous men and women. In fact, it is the hardest job besides being married that you will ever take on. Parenting is not for the faint of heart. It is for men and women who will say, "My children are a priority in my life. I am going to pray for them, and by faith I am going to be the kind of parent that God has called me to be. I am not going to be lazy or slack. I am going to be a person God can look at and say, 'Yes, she is a woman who will raise her children to follow after Me all the days of their lives.'" This is the kind of example I want to be to my children.

I Love This Thing Called Parenting! is the product of over twenty-five years of ministry and twenty years of hands-on training in raising our three children. The principles found in this book are tried and true. Casey and I have used them and seen the success in our own lives and the lives of our children, in addition to those who have been a part of our ministry throughout the years.

I Love This Thing Called Parenting...

I have read dozens of books, listened to hundreds of teaching tapes over the years and talked to many great friends regarding parenting. I have gained invaluable information from them all. Since I do not remember from whom I may have gained a concept or specific words to give credit, I apologize and say, "Thank you for sharing your wisdom and insight!"

There is no such thing as a "perfect" mom. I haven't been a "perfect" mom, but I have learned some great parenting principles through the years of raising my children. Just like you, I am a mom who loves God, loves her children, and is committed to grow in His Word. I live my life in a way that I can say to my children, *Follow me as I follow Christ*.

Wendy Treat

Wendy Treat

Part 1
What Is A Parent?

"Behold children are a heritage from the Lord, The fruit of the womb is His reward."
Psalm 127:3

Chapter 1
Who is this Woman Called *Mom*?

When we become more secure in knowing who we are in Christ, it becomes easier to raise our children to be the strong, secure people God has created them to be.

I Love This Thing Called Parenting...

Things have changed a lot since the parenting days of *Leave It to Beaver*, a hit television show from the early sixties. On *Leave It to Beaver*, the TV family was just so perfect. The mom, *June Cleaver*, cooked dinner every night in a dress while wearing pearls and an apron. She always had dinner on the table at 5:00pm and was never seen with her hair messy or frazzled in any way. She was the *ideal mom* and generations of women used her as their role model.

Of course, most women never attained the perfection shown on *Leave It to Beaver*. It would be impossible even in the best of times. Our world today is vastly different from that of past generations.

Our world has become so complex, with information almost being thrown at us on a daily basis. We can become overloaded with facts, data, ideas, and opinions. How do we know what is right and what is wrong? Sifting through it all can become so overwhelming many of us just give up, flip on the television, and try to forget the whole thing.

The good news is, as Christians we have a "hot line" to *The Source* of every answer. The information we need to make right choices for our families can be found in God's Word. We don't have to look far and wide, sift through the popular ideas of the day, or write a letter to "Dear Abby" to find the answers we need as parents.

First things first.

As parents, the first thing you and I have to know is who *we* are. Galatians 6:4, 9 in The Message Bible says:

> *Make a careful exploration of who you are and the work you have been given, and then sink yourself into that. Don't be impressed with yourself. Don't compare yourself with others. Each of you must take*

responsibility for doing the creative best you can with your own life. So let's not allow ourselves to get fatigued doing good. At the right time we will harvest a good crop if we don't give up, or quit.

In knowing who we are we must recognize our strengths and rejoice in them. God tells us to examine our own strengths, examine our own abilities, know who we are, *and then* we will have rejoicing in ourselves alone, and not in another.

When we become more secure in knowing who we are in Christ, it becomes easier to raise our children to be the strong, secure people God has created them to be. As we recognize our own gifts and abilities, we can then see the gifts in our children. When we begin to see ourselves as God sees us, we can pass on that strength to our children.

Don't compare yourself!

Secondly, the scripture in Galatians teaches us that we need to understand we are not to compare ourselves with others. To compare ourselves with others can open the door for many problems, disappointments, and discouragement.

Many of us moms compare ourselves to the lady next door with our perception of her perfect yard and happy children or we compare ourselves with Aunt Betsy who was practically Betty Crocker in the kitchen. We feel we will never live up to the example set by June Cleaver as the perfect TV mom. We compare and compete until we make ourselves, our husbands, and our children crazy.

Instead of being strengthened with the Word, many times we become strong in our thoughts of: *I can't. It won't work. I'm not good enough.* Gideon said in Judges 6:15 (my paraphrase): "I am weak. I am the least. No, I can't do it, and I'm really nervous about this." Many of us never let God show us our tremendous strengths because all we see are our weaknesses and our failures as compared to what we see in others. We let the spirit of Gideon overcome us in a negative sense.

You have been given the wonderful gift from God to be a parent, but you also have to quit thinking of yourself as weak or not good enough. You have to quit thinking of yourself as the least. You have to examine yourself and realize He has equipped you. He has given you all that you need to raise your children up to love and honor Him.

Don't grow weary!

And finally, the scripture tells us, don't grow weary. As a parent, it is so easy to become discouraged, tired, worn out, and just plain weary. As I've said, parenting is for the courageous. We have to plod on, plod on, plod on. We have to continue to do the right things, speak the Word, teach, train, and love our children. It really will all pay off in the end. Someday, sooner than you think, you will see the results of your labor of love.

Think about who you are in Christ, and then operate in that to the fullest. Take the time to educate yourself to become a skilled mom. Don't compare yourself with others. Soar with the strengths God has put within you. As you learn who you are in Him, you will be given the ability to be a *great* mom.

Questions to Ponder

1. What are your strengths as a parent?

2. Are there any situations or issues that you have given up on? Perhaps you have been overwhelmed or felt inadequate to deal with them.

3. What are you willing to do to change your answer to question #2? (For example: Ask for help? Stop comparing yourself to others?) Look up scriptures that address your situation and who you are in Christ.

For more teaching on knowing who you are in Christ you can order Wendy Treat's book, *Mirror, Mirror On The Wall: Seeing Yourself Through God's Eyes* at www.caseytreat.com.

Chapter 2
Characteristics of a *Great* Mom

When you love
God, your children
will follow your
example.

A *great* mom doesn't just talk the talk, she also walks the walk. She is a strong, positive example for her children. She influences her children by her godly lifestyle. She is a major key in influencing the decisions that are important to their future success. She lives a life they want to emulate. A great mom not only desires to influence her own children, but also sees the value of influencing those around her. A great mom is a mentor and role model.

As parents, we are the primary example of Christ to our children on the earth. As an example to my children and as a woman of God, I want to walk in the fruit of the Spirit, which is listed in Galatians 5:22-23: *But the fruit of the Spirit is, love, joy, peace, longsuffering, kindness, goodness, faithfulness, gentleness, self-control. Against such there is no law.*

I want my children to know that Jesus is real by my lifestyle. Ask yourself, "Am I walking in the fruit of the Spirit? Am I walking in kindness? Am I walking in forgiveness? Am I walking in joy? Or, am I letting the sadness and stress of life settle in on me?"

What kind of example are you?

Are you setting a good example? When your child does a childish thing, do you smile, or do you always get irritated? Do you let joy reside in your heart and in your household, or do you always pick, pick, pick?

If your child acts in a childish behavior, yet he or she isn't being disobedient, and you say, "Stop it. Don't do that. I am so tired. You are driving me crazy," that is *not* walking in the fruit of the Spirit. That is allowing anger, hostility, and irritation to rise up in you. In a few years your children will talk like you talk. They will use the mannerisms you use. They will walk like you walk. I decided a long time ago, *if my children are going to copy me – if everyone is going to see all the little things I do – I'd better make sure that what my children see is a good example.*

What is your example as a driver? Usually I drive the speed limit, but my kids would say, "Mom, go faster," and I would say, "Look at the speedometer. See how fast I am going?" "Yes." "Well, that's how fast I am going to go." You have to think bigger than your own desires and do things Christ's way.

When you are talking to someone on the phone, responding to people in the grocery store, or working at your job, are you a woman of integrity? Do your children ever see you reading the Bible? Do your children hear you praying? What does church mean to you? Do you go to church and then on the way home whine and complain: "I didn't get out of the parking lot fast enough." "Did you see that children's worker and the usher who were not very nice to me?" "They sang that stupid song again."

A lot of adults complain about the preacher too; then they wonder why, when their kids are teenagers they don't want to go to church with them. Why? You have not been an example of a person who honors God, honors the people who serve in the Kingdom of God, and honors the gift of the pastoral role that God has given to the church.

What kind of example are you in the physical realm? Do you say, "Hey, throw me a bag of chips and a pop?" Are you an example of a woman who has discipline in her life? Are you going to make some hard choices that may not be fun, because you want to live a long, prosperous life? Occasionally you can eat whatever you want – I'm just talking about making choices on a regular, consistent basis. I am talking about what you *practice* in the physical realm.

What is your practice in your appearance and how you care for yourself? What do you practice in the soul realm – in your mind, emotions, and will? What do you allow to be viewed on TV in your house? What do you allow into your mind? What do you allow yourself to listen to? What do you allow yourself to be involved with? These are things for you to consider when we talk of being an example.

I want my example to be like Christ. That means I have to make certain choices. "I will not do this. I will not watch that. I will not listen to this." You want to be an example for your children so they can follow after you as you follow Christ. Your children will notice the choices you make.

Ponder your words and actions.

I love Proverbs 4:26: ***Ponder the path of your feet.*** As moms, we must speak with wisdom, we must ponder the options, and we must consider our words so when we interact with our children, we aren't too quick with our response. We shouldn't just shoot something off the top of our head, but first ponder what we really want to communicate to them. Think: Have I heard these words from my child before? Why are they going in this direction? Has something happened around them or in their life that is causing this behavior?

Don't be like a Mack truck and roll over your child's emotions and feelings because he may have said something wrong! Instead of being a lazy mom by saying to your child, "That's not true. Hush! Go do your homework," you should ponder, and think, *Is there something that I am missing?* **Consider. Think.**

Maybe your children are at a certain age when there are all kinds of emotions going on. Maybe your son just got rejected from a school team. Maybe there are things going on you may not be aware of. You need to consider, ponder, and think, *Okay, there might be some other issue involved in this.*

Maybe you have a third grader and someone called her "buck teeth," so her emotions are raw. She shouts at you, "You don't love me." She's not really saying YOU don't love her. She is communicating that she is feeling bad about a situation at school. This is when you can be a strong, godly mom by saying, "Sweetheart, I love you." Speak words of life into your children right away. Love covers a multitude of sins, and maybe sin was committed against your child in words or actions.

Touch your child. Speak words of life to her. Comment on different actions you see in her that are good and that are godly. Make sure you notice her. "I noticed how sweet you were to your brother." Or, "I noticed how you really took care to comb your hair. It looks great." Speak life instead of death over your children and practice words of love.

Learn how to be gentle.

The scripture says a gentle answer will turn away wrath. Learn how to use gentleness in your communication. Learn how to slow down. Learn how to turn off the TV. If you are reading a book, close the book. If you have something on the stove and you have to watch it, turn it off and turn toward your child. Give them the feeling that, "You are the one I am valuing. You are it!" Then at the right time you can say, "You know I love you. Is there something else going on?" You can bring them to the next level of getting help for whatever is going on in their lives. Make room for your child to visit and talk with you. I love my own private time, but when my children come in, my private time is over so I can pay attention to their needs.

When I decided to follow the Word, I stopped acting in a worldly way by demanding my own time. I decided, "That's it, get out of the way, Wendy Louise!" Act in the right way and give priority to other people in your life, and the most valuable ones are in your own household.

Growing up in my home, there was no physical touch until I hit my teenage years. My mom then must have heard someone teach about the importance of physically touching your children and hugging them. Seriously, I had not experienced that from my mom until I was about thirteen years old. My dad had always been physical in hugging us, but not my mom. When she first touched me, I remember thinking, "What are you doing? Get your hand off of my arm!" I can remember the moment my mom changed, and it influenced me. So regardless of your children's ages, when you receive truth it is never too late to be an example of that truth. As you begin to live it out in your life, it will produce fruit in their lives.

Deuteronomy 6:5 says: *You shall love the Lord your God with all your heart, with all your soul, and with all your strength.* To love the Lord with all of your soul means to love Him with your mind, your will, and your emotions. This means that in the course of becoming a great mom, we must submit our will, our emotions, and our thoughts to what God says above everything else.

We have a choice of what kind of woman we want to be. We can either obey what the Word of God has to say, or we can continue to say, "I'm not going to submit to that. I am not going to give God the number one spot. I want to do it my way." Can God say of you, "I know My daughter. She will raise her children in the way they should go"? That's what I want God to be able to say about me in the area of influencing my children.

Teach and train with "real life" situations.

Deuteronomy 6: 6-7 goes on to say: *And these words which I command you today shall be in your heart. You shall teach them diligently to your children, and shall talk of them when you sit in your house, when you walk by the way, when you lie down, and when you rise up.*

These verses give great accountability to us as moms. Many think, *I'll take my kids to church and they will teach them.* Why do people simply drop their kids off at church? Where did we get that idea? How many parents take their kids to church, leave them there, and don't go themselves? That does not work! When *you* love God, your children will follow your example.

If I say to my children, "You go to church," but I don't go myself, why would they want to go? In most cases, children won't do what you say, but they will do what you do. They will follow your example, not just the words you speak. I'm not saying they will clearly make a decision not to go to church because Mom and Dad don't go. But you are showing them by your example the value of loving God and going to church or not going to church. As great moms, we have to show by our own example the value of loving God.

It is very clear from the verses we read in Deuteronomy that God does not delegate the responsibility of training your children to the church, a Bible class, or a Christian school. It is not up to the pastor to make sure your children are taught how to live out the principles found in the Word of God. It is your responsibility as a parent to teach them how to live the principles found in the Bible.

A great mom is the trainer and the instructor of her children. We are the ones who need to take the mantle and the wonderful responsibility of being our child's trainer. Are we afraid to speak with our children about morals, character, and godly principles? Are we too busy with living to spend time teaching our children the values of life? God puts a lot of trust in us as moms, but it is our choice to step up to the plate to teach and train our children.

We are to teach God's Word diligently to our children. "Diligently" means regularly. *...and you shall talk of them when you sit in your house, when you walk by the way, when you lie down, and when you rise up* (Deuteronomy 6:7).

Several years ago, I spoke to some young people who hated their family devotions. The children were made to sit around the table while their father read the Bible. As he read to them he would fall asleep. As soon as he fell asleep, the kids would sneak off. They learned how to disregard and disrespect the Bible because their own father did not love the Lord with all his heart. He did not show respect for God's Word, and he lost the respect of his children.

What are you teaching? Are you conversing with your children about the Bible? Make God's Word a part of your lifestyle, speaking of it when you are walking, talking, and lying down. This means that you should visit with your kids and talk about the principles and the character of God throughout your daily life.

How did Jesus teach the principles of God? As He walked along, He would say, "Look at the tree," and teach a lesson. He would use the wind and the storm as examples. He used what was around Him. That's how He taught what He believed. You and I are to be creative thinking moms as we talk about all the things of God with our children.

When my children were younger, I taught them as we drove in the car. Instead of zoning out or listening to loud music I would use these moments to talk about the things around us. When I drove around a certain bend in our road on the way home, a beautiful view of Mt. Rainier was often right in front of us. As we looked at Mt. Rainier I would say, "God created the heavens and the earth. He created the beauty all around us." I took the moment to reinforce the greatness of God and His creation. I was teaching my children to appreciate beauty and also the vastness of all God has created for us to enjoy.

On many a foggy day we couldn't see the mountain at all. That big, huge mountain would simply be gone! I'd say, "Look! We know the mountain is there, don't we?" "Yeah." "But we can't see it today." "Yeah." "That's like faith. When God gives us a promise from the Word, we can't always see it right away, but it's still there." Then the next day we would come around the corner and the sun would be shining and we would be able to see Mt. Rainier. I would say, "It's there! Now, it was there yesterday too, but we just couldn't see it."

I have another favorite corner on the road to our home. Before we get up to our house, you can see a valley below filled with all sorts of color. There are pumpkins in the fall. There is a variety of colorful flowers in the spring. Sometimes during the rainy months it looks like a lake! I would love to point out the changes of each season to my children. As moms we can use natural beauty to teach our children God's principles of life everywhere we go.

I think that too many moms get in the car with their kids, sit down for dinner with their kids, have breakfast with their kids, or are around their kids, and all we think about is, "Did you comb your hair right? Did you brush your teeth? Did you do your homework?" Those are important issues, because we are all to train them how to live in the sense of being ready for life, but often we forget the most valuable part of life: training our children about the immense goodness and majesty of God!

When we would look at all the colors in the valley while driving to our house, I'd say, "Look at all the colors! That's like God's Kingdom. There are all kinds of people, all different colors of people, and they have many types of talents."

When you're teaching them, use words that don't sound like a Bible lesson. Use the right words so your kids don't say, "Oh, Mom. You're teaching us again." I always asked my kids questions. As they grew older we were able to carry on some great conversations. I encouraged them to bring up spiritual stories and figure out how to use them to understand people today and to value the beauty of God's creation.

Questions of the heart.

Do you spend time just visiting with your children –

having conversations with them – caring about who they are? As parents we can say, "Oh, aren't you looking good?" "Isn't that a beautiful dress?" "Your hair is so pretty." It's so easy to look at the outside. But we don't ask questions of the heart as easily. We don't take the time to talk with them. Try saying things such as, "How are you doing, Honey?" "What's going on with you?" "Did you learn a new song? Go ahead and sing it to me."

When you are teaching your children using objects and stories and all the things of life, tell them stories about your own life. Share with them some of your weaknesses. Share the things that you have had to go through in your life. Share some of your pain relating to the situations that happened when you were young.

Casey was arrested for drugs as a teenager, so we have always talked openly and honestly with our kids about why he started using drugs, the choices he made along the way, and the problems, pains, and hurts that resulted.

I've shared honestly with my children about failures in my own life. When I talk to my daughter about different issues, I'll say, "Truthfully, my mom never talked to me about any of this, so how am I doing? Am I talking too much or not enough?" She'll say, "Mom, you are doing a good job" and I'll say, "Okay, just keep me informed, Sweetheart." I want to be an honest mom.

Listen, ponder, and think.

Go for a walk with your children to change the environment so you can have a conversation with them. A godly mom listens, ponders, and thinks about her children. Many of us moms get into such a routine of life that we do the same thing repeatedly. Sometimes we don't take time to ponder, *how am I going to help my child? Do they need to see something different? How can I reach them? What is it that they need?* It could be that they need to be taken out to lunch so they can have that "alone" time with you. Sometimes they need personal attention.

As a great mom, we need to also deal with the issues of the spirit and soul – not just the body. Today the world looks on the outside, and that's all they see. Maybe as Christian women we are sometimes just as guilty, because all we see is how cute our kids are. We need to go deeper than that.

As women, either we will train our children by the world's way or by the Word's way. The world is fighting for our children's hearts, and it is fighting for your heart and mine. But Proverbs 22:6 gives us a wonderful promise if we will believe it, speak it, and act upon it: *Train up a child in the way he should go, and when he is old he will not depart from it.*

Remember, I said at the beginning we are not always perfect. A great mom often does not always feel great. She doesn't always feel successful. In fact, we often wonder, doubt, and believe someone else could probably raise our kids better than we can (I sure have at times). Yet the fact that you are taking the time to read and study to become a *better* mom proves my point; a great mom isn't perfect but she is someone who is doing all she can to learn, putting herself through the work of changing and challenging herself to be the best she can be.

A *great* mom is one who puts God first in her own life and is a strong, godly example for her children. A *great* mom is willing to live her life in a way that her children will choose to follow her as she follows Christ.

Questions to Ponder

1. Is God number one in your life? If so, keep living the life! If not, what will you do to let Him be number one?

2. What kind of parent do you want to be? (Consider what kind of example you want to set in your spiritual life, soul/mind/will/emotional life, physical life, financial life, and social life.)

3. Which area will you start to work on first?

Chapter 3
The Influence of a *Great* Dad

If you have more than one child, you are going to have to figure out more than one way of parenting.

I Love This Thing Called Parenting...

For I have known him, in order that he may command his children and his household after him, that they keep the way of the Lord, to do righteousness and justice...

Genesis 18:19a

A great dad is one who has his household in order. He can command his household...which simply means to lead your family into the ways of God. When I think about our society today, I have a question for you men: "Does God know you? Does God know *you*, or does He only know your *momma*...uh, I mean your *wife*?"

I have heard men say, "My momma was a praying woman, and she prayed for me. My grandmother prayed for me." Traditionally it has been the mommas and grandmothers who have prayed and stood in the gap, but men are also to pray and stand in the gap. Prayer is not a "girls only" activity. God didn't say, "Women's work will be cleaning, cooking, and praying. I will have the men only be the providers and protectors."

I would love to someday see a brother stand up when he wins the Super Bowl and say, "Thank you, Dad, for praying for me." That would show strength. It would represent a nation that is strong, because when men are strong for God, the rest of the family will be strong, too. There is a desire within a woman to follow a strong man – a man who honors God – a man who will say, "I'm not ashamed to be a man who loves and honors God." Women will follow a man like that. Although many women are strong, they love to follow a man of whom God says, "I know him."

Men need to take on the wonderful mantle, honor, and job of leading their family. Many have given up that responsibility. They expect the *mommas* to do it, or the church to do it. Does someone else have control of the spiritual training of your household?

Let's look again at the verse quoted at the beginning of the chapter, *For I have known him, in order that he may command his children and his household after him, that they keep the way of the Lord, to do righteousness and justice...* (Genesis 18:19a)

God knew Sarah was a strong woman, but He didn't go to Sarah in Genesis and say, "I know Sarah. She will command her family after Me." God went to the man, Abraham, and said, "He will command his family after Me and he will lead his family." I love what He adds at the end of the verse...*that they keep the way of the Lord, to do righteousness and justice...*

Righteousness is doing the right thing. Justice deals with integrity and the quality of being honorable and living correctly in the sight of God. Men, you are commanded to lead your family in this way. My goal is to stir you fathers up to be the kind of men God has called you to be. I want to encourage you men to build and strengthen yourselves in the things of God.

You have to fight for godliness!

Men of God, you have to fight for the way of the Lord! Other things and other desires will try to take priority. There are always things that try to take up your time – with work probably being the number one issue that will take you away from your family. As you start to succeed financially, beware of getting caught up in wanting more stuff and neglecting your God-given priority. Frankly, we can never get enough "stuff." It's so easy to get caught up in getting the *things* of life and allowing them to become our god.

The Word teaches us that when we put God's house first place in our lives, He will take care of our house (Haggai 1:1-11). When we believe the Word of God we can have all our needs met, and we can raise our families to love and honor God.

There are many qualities that a great father will possess. I would like to list a few of these qualities by using an acronym for the word, *father*:

F *Fear of the Lord*
A *Attuned*
T *There*
H *Husband who loves his wife*
E *Example*
R *Rich in the things of God*

"F" – Fear of the Lord

Fear of the Lord means "to honor and reverence God". Too many people do not honor and reverence God. Because we don't, we make our *own* choices and think we can do whatever we want to do at any time. We don't have a sense of reverence for God – the One who opens blind eyes, and heals the sick – He Who loved and yet gave His only Son.

Many of us live our lives based upon our own whims and desires. We base raising our children and leading our family on what is comfortable. We do what we want to do and what feels good instead of basing our choices on what the Word of God says.

We will all stand before God some day and give an account of our lives. We will need to give an account of every word that came out of our mouths. We will give an account of all the actions we did – or didn't do – during our life. Husbands will give an account of their relationships with their wives, and then give an account of how they led their children.

Men, you may be thinking, *Oh no, I want to talk about all the businesses I started, all the things I purchased, all the games I played.* God says, "Hello! I don't give two hoots about your business." He is not impressed with how far a man got in his company and or much overtime was put in. He wants to know how husbands and fathers influenced their wives and children.

We work hard every single day. God has given us life and wants us to live in abundance on this earth, but earth life is short while heaven life is immeasurable. Heaven life is forever. We have to pick the right priorities during our short earth life. Men, usually more than women, need to recognize that their number one priority is to lead and love their family – their wives and children – in the fear of the Lord.

Fathers need to decide to be a dad who doesn't skip out on church, doesn't skip prayer, doesn't skip reading the Bible and doesn't skip honoring and serving the King of kings and the Lord of lords. They need to decide that their household will be one that reverences and fears the Lord.

When you know God and walk in the fear of the Lord, you will have your priorities in line. As a godly man, lead in the spiritual battles of your household, it brings strength and security into the hearts of your wife and children. God will bless and prosper you, spirit, soul, and body, as you put Him first place in your life.

"A" – Attuned

Fathers are to be tuned in or attuned to their children. Proverbs 22:6 (Amplified Bible) says: *Train up a child in the way he should go [and in keeping with his individual gift or bent], and when he is old he will not depart from it.*

As a father, have you considered the uniqueness and the difference of each of the children who are in your household and have you spent the time to find out who each of them really are? Do you know what is important to *them*?

There are certain godly characteristics we want our children to have: love, joy, peace, kindness, gentleness, longsuffering, faithfulness, goodness, and self-control. These fruits of the Spirit are the godly qualities we want to put within each of our children. As we teach, train, and lead our children through life, we spend time showing them how to live a life that shows the fruit of God's love in their lives.

But, just like each one of the fruits of the Spirit is different, each of our children's personalities are also different. Our children are not clones of one another. And guess what, God doesn't want them to be the same. He expects them to be different because He gave each one of them the different gifting and talents they possess. The more children we have, the more gifting and talents we will have represented in our households.

It can be slightly dismaying the first time you realize your second child doesn't do things the way your first child did. You suddenly realize the same kind of discipline doesn't work with this one. As a parent, have you had one of those moments when you look at one of your children and think, *I am the same parent. I raised you the same as the other one. Why am I not getting the same results?* One is not evil and the other one good. Sometimes it just feels like that because as parents we like the road of least resistance. Some kids are simply easier to raise than others.

If you have more than one child, you are going to have to figure out more than one way of parenting. You have to take the time with each child to discover their strengths and weaknesses. You need to learn about and figure out who is this amazing gift from God. Then you must do everything within your ability as a parent to help your child be all that God has called them to be.

Being attuned to your children means knowing them and making the effort to understand the gifts and callings in their lives. As a dad you need to take the time to appreciate the differences in your children, and not just assume they are "just like dear old dad." What if you were the school jock, but your son is gifted in music or academics. Being in tune with and appreciating your child's personality and giftings will enable you to go from being a clueless dad to being a *great* dad.

"T" – There

Very simply, fathers need to be there, in the presence of their children. Watch them. Talk with them. Have dinner with them. Have breakfast with them when possible, and just be around them. Children need their fathers to applaud them and be supportive. Look at their school work and appreciate what is happening in their life. Nothing can replace the time dads take to spend with their children.

If your children are involved in sports make a plan to be at the games to watch, applaud, laugh, share their sorrow, and experience the moment with them. They may never remember the details of the game, or even the coach's name, but they will always remember if you were there to be a part of their special moment.

I am not talking about a legalistic rule that you have to be at each and every event or game. You may not physically be able to attend every event. But, if you cannot be at a special event, show your interest in their event and let them know of your disappointment at not being able to attend. In the morning before they go to school you can say, "I know you are doing (such and such) today. I'm really excited. We'll talk about it tonight when I see you." Then later reconnect and ask, "How did it go?" Whenever possible go to the event, be there. Watch them and be involved with what they are doing and be their best supporter.

"H" – Husband who loves his wife

A *great* dad loves his children's momma. A word of wisdom for you husbands; when you get home from work, go to your wife *first*. She is your priority. She is the one who will be there when all of your kids are grown up and gone. Look for her first, and wives, don't be too busy. Don't give off the signal, "I'm busy. Don't touch me. Don't hug me." It is really up to both the husband and the wife to work at keeping your marriage strong by making your spouse your priority.

It is so important for your kids to know that you love each other. Let them see you communicate with each other. Hug and kiss, even if it embarrasses your kids (G-rated, of course!) and love each other. Our kids are used to seeing Casey and me hugging and kissing. We kiss and hug in front of them on purpose. We want them to see that we love each other.

Parents who love each other bring a great deal of security into their children's hearts. When they see you kissing and hugging, they are going to say, "Yuck...gross...stop it!" But inside they will feel happy because they know you like each other. They won't really understand the thought process, but in their minds they know that parents who like each other stay together. And parents who stay together bring peace and security to the lives of their children.

"E" – Example

What kind of example are you – spirit, soul, and body – for your children? What kind of example are you spiritually? What kind of an example are you in the soul realm? What kind of an example are you physically? When your child looks at you, what does he (or she) see? Your children will follow your example. As a spiritual man, do your children know you read the Bible? Do they listen to you pray? Casey and I believe in praying as a family, but we don't say, "This is the time we have to have prayer every day." We both regularly pray with our family, and every single day we pray with each of our children individually.

One day Casey was praying and one of our kids said, "Dad, will you stop praying?" Another child said, "No, you don't want him to quit praying. He's praying for us, you know." I thought, *that is great and that is the truth.*

Do your children see you as a spiritual dad whose

priority is reading the Bible? Are you involved with church? This is the spiritual example we want our children to have in the long term of their life. As godly fathers, don't just let the women take the lead in the spiritual life of your family. Be a man who leads!

Are you an example in your soul realm? Your soul is your mind, your emotions and your will. Do you love to read and learn? Are you seeking spiritual growth? Do you get excited when you learn new things and share them with your family? Being a great dad includes giving your children an example of someone who loves to study, read, and learn new things. Children will be better students when they see that learning is a privilege and a joy in life.

In your emotional realm, are you a person who is given to depression, fear, anxiety, or anger? Or are you renewing the spirit of your mind so that your soul is peaceful, gentle, kind, and full of faith? Do you react with anger while incorrectly judging a situation, or do you take the time to speak calmly, ask questions, and even pray before making harsh decisions? Are you quick to say, "You're grounded!" Or do you take a moment to assess the situation before speaking your mind?

In the physical realm, are you one who says, "Get me a beer" while you sit on the couch all night watching sports? Or are you a dad who sets a godly example for your household by eating right, exercising, and being active around the house? Do you set the example at dinner time by eating healthy foods? Do you take the time to keep your body in good condition by exercising on a regular basis so you will live a long life?

A *great* dad lives his life as a strong example to his

children. I don't mean to say that you need to be perfect, but that you are consciously making the best choices in every situation and living in a manner that reflects Christ in your actions. Your actions do speak louder than your words, and you are the one your children are looking to as a role-model and godly example for their lives.

"R" – Rich in the things of God

Beloved, I pray that you may prosper in all things and be in health, just as your soul prospers (III John 2).

Men, you do not have to tell a woman to submit to you if you are a man who loves God. Children will not depart from God when fathers live as a godly example for them. Within the heart of every woman is the desire to follow a righteous man. Every child has the desire to honor, love, and follow after the ways of their dad. You are their hero, the man they look up to and want to emulate above all others. Be the man God has called you to be…a *great* dad!

Questions to Ponder

1. As the father, have you taken on the responsibility of leading your family, or have you let others like your wife, parents, the church, or school lead for you?

2. Think about how you have set your priorities. Where does God show up on your list? How are you doing at keeping Him number one?

3. Consider the qualities of a father listed in this chapter. Which areas are you strongest in and which are you willing to work on?

Chapter 4
The Word of God View vs. The World View

God has given us instruction in His Word on how to raise our children to love and honor Him.

So God created man in His own image; in the image of God He created him; male and female He created them. Then God blessed them, and God said to them, "Be fruitful and multiply; fill the earth and subdue it; have dominion over the fish of the sea, over the birds of the air, and over every living thing that moves on the earth."
Genesis 1:27, 28

The bull's-eye of God's plan for the family is that there is *a husband* and *a wife*. In today's world, it has become popular for single men and women to adopt children. Their attitude is, "Hey, don't tell me I can't have a child." But I want to say, "Hello! The Bible clearly says a husband and a wife are to be fruitful and multiply. The Bible also says a child is to honor his *parents*." So the bull's-eye, the best, of God's design is that there is a mom and a dad.

Why do you suppose it was important enough to God that He set up the family this way? I believe He knew the tremendous benefit our children would receive from each parent. Simply put, a woman is not a man and a man is not a woman. It is not possible for me, as a mom, to give my children the male part of parenting. I know it is not politically correct to say that, but it's the truth. I'm not going to try to be a male role-model for my children. I don't have that ability. I am going to be a strong female role-model in their lives because that is who God created me to be.

God has given the job of fathering to the males of this earth – the unique gifting and masculinity of the male is an important part of raising healthy children. God took the woman out of the man and gave her the uniqueness of her femininity to bring balance and completeness to the family. Each of us has an important role in the overall raising of our children.

In parenting, the ideal plan is that there is a mom and a dad to raise their children. But even in biblical times that wasn't always so. If you are a single mom, you can be a godly parent and raise your children to walk strong in the Lord. Timothy, a great pastor and leader at the beginning of the Church, was raised by his godly mother and grandmother.

I know that many single parents struggle with feeling they don't have God's best and therefore their children will become less than they should or could be. I will further address the whole issue of "the guilty mom," single parenting, and blended families in upcoming chapters. Keep reading and you will see that God wasn't caught off-guard by your situation. He has the answer for every situation in which we find ourselves.

Abraham: God's first parenting role-model.

God spoke of Abraham in Genesis18:19a: *For I have known him, in order that he may command his children and his household after him, that they keep the way of the Lord, to do righteousness and justice...*

It is apparent from these verses that God saw Abraham as a godly parent. He had some pretty amazing things to say about how Abraham ran his household. We can use these same guidelines today in measuring ourselves as parents. Ask yourself these questions taken from the verse above:

- Does God know me?
- Do I give myself to the instruction of the Word?

- Do I lead my family in keeping God's ways?
- Do I practice righteousness in my home?

Until you have made the decision to live God's way, learn His Word, and follow Him, you will be double-minded in all of your ways. I see many people who say they know God and are walking in the Word, yet they want to keep their hand in the world. They claim to be Christians, yet want to continue to live like the world.

I challenge you to ask yourself if you have truly chosen to follow Christ. If you haven't yet decided to live fully for Christ, why not do that now? You have to realize that the way of the world is hard. That path will lead you and your children to death and destruction.

My grandfather was a pastor. At one point there was a man attending the church whose job was to drive a beer truck. My grandfather thought about it and said, "This is not a righteous job because it produces evil and problems in people's lives." He wouldn't let the man become a member of his church, although he allowed him to attend.

My grandfather took some flack for his decision, but his stand was based upon the Word. He said, "No, the Bible says to do honest work and it's not honest work if it brings destruction into the lives of people." It wasn't easy for him, but he chose what the Bible said over what would be easy.

You might say, "Oh, well, that's no big deal!" But, when I was a teenager, my mom told me this story and the decision Grandpa had made. There came a time before I was saved when I was seriously considering drinking and this example came to me. I remember thinking about it and I knew I could not do it. The actions of my grandfather had a great impact on my life even though it was many, many years later. This type of training is a generational blessing for our children. Because my grandfather stood for righteousness, I also made the stand to live for God's ways. I look at myself now, years later, and realize there were many other choices my grandparents made that my parents followed and then I, in turn, have also followed. I have the benefit of generations of godliness to follow.

Does God know you?

Does God know who you are? Does He know that you will train your children to follow Him and keep His ways? Have you considered that the choices you are making today will affect generations to come? I was reading a study about this not long ago. It was a comparative study of two families and how each family's choices affected future generations. One followed an ungodly man who did not believe in Jesus Christ and who refused to take his children to church. The other study followed the family of the great preacher, Jonathan Edwards.

The generations that followed the ungodly man's family produced prisoners, prostitutes, and alcoholics – generations of people making no positive contribution to society. However, in the generations that followed Jonathan Edwards, who loved the Lord and took his children to church every Sunday, there were ministers, university presidents and professors, authors, congressmen, and one vice-president of our nation. His descendants contributed immeasurably to society!

We must ask ourselves, "What kind of person do I want to be? What kind of descendants do I want in the generations following me?" We have to think bigger than ourselves. Think not just about today, not even of tomorrow, not even of a year from now, but in terms of ten, twenty, thirty, forty, fifty, and more years from now. What are you going to see in the future on your family tree?

Undoubtedly there were challenges in my grandparents' lives, yet they remained godly. Both sides of my parents' families made the decision to live for God and stood strong for righteousness. I can't begin to know all the seeds that were planted for me or the influence they have had in my life. This motivates me to really love God and be a person of whom God can say, "Wendy knows Me. She knows who I am. She understands the principles of My Word, and she will train her children up in the way that they should go."

A world of difference!

There is a definite difference between the world view of child training and the Word view. The person with a world view never wants to "repress" a child. They want to live from reward to reward and from incentive to incentive. They don't want to impose their values on a child, because basically that child is so sweet, so good, so perfect, and so innocent they want them to be able to make their own choices. A person with a strong world view says, "Goodness will come out of the heart of every child." That sounds so good...but, it is not so.

Years ago I knew a Christian woman who obviously held the world view of child training. I watched this woman and I remember thinking, *it is so sad that she would say, "I want to come to church, but I don't want to impose my views on my kids. They are such good kids that I know they will make good choices."*

I tried to help her recognize that the way of the world is a path of destruction and foolishness. That foolishness is bound up in the hearts of our children. They don't know what they are supposed to believe. They don't know how they are supposed to walk. Unless we teach them, our children don't know how to make right choices.

This is a simple example: If you take your four-year-old child out to a fancy restaurant and you have all those forks and spoons above the plate and beside the plate, does that child know which fork to use? They don't know which fork to pick up if you have more than one set before them. Remember, the world says goodness is within the child and he is brilliant. No, they don't know which fork to use. They don't know which fork to use, any more than they know what to believe.

Just because a person is born doesn't mean they will love God. Children don't know that foolishness is bound up in their hearts. They don't get it. Just like you have to teach them what fork to use, you have to teach them about God. You have to teach them how to act towards people. You have to teach them the fruit of the Spirit: love, joy, peace, longsuffering, kindness, goodness, faithfulness, gentleness, and self-control. You have to train them up in the way they should go. You can't just think they will know what to do naturally.

Psalm 127:1-5 teaches us:

Unless the Lord builds the house, they labor in vain who build it; unless the Lord guards the city, the watchman stays awake in vain. It is vain for you to rise up early, to sit up late, to eat the bread of sorrows; for so He gives His beloved sleep. Behold, children are a heritage from the Lord, the fruit of the womb is a reward. Like arrows in the hand of a warrior, so are the children of one's youth. Happy is the man who has his quiver full of them; they shall not be ashamed, but shall speak with their enemies in the gate.

You have to make a choice. What kind of parent are you going to be? Are you going to put the Word first, or are you going to train your children the world's way?

God made us individual and unique!

The world will teach you how to train your children through TV programs that ridicule the Word and ridicule discipline, training, and manners. They ridicule the thought of children having a moral code built into their hearts. The world says, (my paraphrase), "Make everybody exactly the same." Yet the Word says, my paraphrase, train up a child in the individual bent of who he is and when he is old, he will not depart from it.

The Bible also teaches in I Corinthians, Chapter 12 that there are diversities of gifts in the Body of Christ and together we make up a whole unit. Each individual represents a different part of the Body of Christ, such as the ears, nose, knees, and toes are all different parts in a natural body. There are different kinds of giftings, but the world wants you to train your children up the same, like robots.

I don't want my three children to be the same. They have different strengths and weaknesses. We work with their weaknesses so they aren't pulled into a negative realm, and we work with their strengths to help them become all that God has called them to be.

I've seen TV shows where little children act like brats. They defy their parents and are rebellious against them. They yell at their parents, "I don't like you." Then they go hide in their room and the parents say, "I don't want to hurt them." I want say to those parents, "Foolishness is bound up in the heart of that child. He doesn't want to rebel. That child needs to be taught not to rebel because rebellion brings dissatisfaction and a separation from love."

When you let a child rebel and they are not corrected, they begin to feel very insecure because the boundaries are gone. They begin to question, "What do I do? How am I supposed to act?" They become insecure and in turn their actions and attitudes gain momentum in a negative way. Most children won't sit themselves down, analyze the situation, and correct their own behavior. They need you to help them and train them in the way they should go.

Like arrows in the hand of a warrior, so are the children of one's youth (Psalm 127:4). I can't imagine a warrior who did not work hard. You have to know that a warrior works at perfecting his skills. He practices over and over again. He works hours upon hours, learning how to do battle. God likens your children to arrows in the hand of a warrior. As parents we must practice. We must train. We must develop. We must learn. We must continue to get better until we know how to shoot and hit the target well. It doesn't happen by chance. You do not raise godly children by chance. You work at it. You make choices for God. You make choices that are tough.

As a godly parent, you learn what the Word says. You put aside your old beliefs and even the way you were raised – not dishonoring your parents but recognizing that

you may have to put away how your parents trained you because it was worldly thinking, not Word thinking.
The ways of the world.

God has given us instruction in His Word on how to raise our children to love and honor Him. The world has also set a standard for what they see as successful parenting skills. There are three different styles of raising children which we see in the world today: The Liberal, The Disciplinarian, and The Double-Minded.

1. The Liberal:

There are those who have a liberal or worldly view of child training. These are the ones who say we should never repress or frustrate a child and never, ever impose our values upon him. Instead, we train him to live for rewards and incentives and allow him to make his own decisions.

A few years ago a sheriff's office in Texas came up with some rules of "How to Raise a *Juvenile Delinquent*." Included in these rules were:

1. Begin with infancy and give the child everything he wants. This will assure him that the world owes him a living.
2. Pick up everything he leaves lying around. This will teach him that he can always throw his responsibilities off on others.
3. Take his side against neighbors, teachers, and policemen. They are all prejudiced against your child. He has a free spirit and he is never wrong.
4. Prepare yourself for a life of grief.

These rules express the liberal point of view in raising children and the rewards that follow. Sadly, we see too many children today who are raised in this manner.

Many believe children should be allowed to do what is right for them and they will evolve into the person they are meant to be if left alone and encouraged to "think outside the box" and "be all that they can be." This kind of thinking does not line up with what the Bible teaches us. The Bible says we are to have the mind of Christ, and set our minds on things above, not on things on this earth. The Bible teaches we are to respect those in authority over us, which is the opposite of the liberal point of view.

2. The Disciplinarian:

The disciplinarian deals with the command mentality or military style of child training. "Do this. Do that. Sit down. Stand up. Walk. Obey me the first time. If you don't obey me right now, I'm going to discipline you. Snap that bed tight and fold in those sheets. Stand up tall."

This is a very extreme type of teaching and training of your children. Many people in the world think this is the way we Christians teach our children. They stereotype Christians as mean people who are always saying no and finding evil in everything. They look at us as the extreme disciplinarian type of people, which is not true. It might be true of *religious* parents, but it's not true of *Christian* parents. "Christian" means to follow Christ and the Word of God, not a set of rules and regulations set up by man.

3. The Double-Minded:

In this type of child training, there is no set pattern or plan of how to be a parent. They will sometimes be very liberal in their responses, and then turn around with a list of rules and regulations a mile long. Their parenting guidelines change from day to day, and from situation to situation. There is no rhyme or reason for the decisions they make and their children never know what to expect.

Usually this type of parent does not know what the Word of God says. This can be dangerous, because they don't take the time to re-examine what has worked, or has not worked, what is biblical, or is not biblical. If it works for them, they don't challenge it. They just accept it all – hook, line, and sinker – not realizing that they were taught some things that were not biblical and were not truth.

Re-examine the principles of God's Word.

I would challenge you to set all of your child raising beliefs aside and then re-examine them by lining them up with the Word of God. Ask yourself, is it worldly or is it the Word? Is it just the way I was raised or is it what God teaches me to do?

Another thing that affects how we train our children is if we were abused or hurt in the past. This includes yelling, screaming, and neglect. As a child, you may have had to chart your own course. If there was violence in your home when you were growing up, it is common to teach and train your children out of fear – fear that you would hurt your child or that you would go overboard as a disciplinarian.

Instead of using a biblical view of raising your children, many choose to take a liberal viewpoint: "I will never lay a hand on my children. I'll never tell them what to do. I'll never demand or command. I'm not going to boss them around. That's what I had to live with. It was horrible. I hated it."

So what do we do? We raise our children based on, "I hated what happened to me, so I will not do anything like that at all," not realizing that some of the things *were correct* – not all of it was wrong.

I want to encourage you to look at *truth* instead of,

"How was I raised?" "What were the things that were put within me?" If a disciplinarian lifestyle is what you came from and you hated it, you will most likely go with total liberalism, and that isn't right either.

Many people who were raised in total liberalism, with no spankings, rules, or boundaries, decide to lay down the law to their children. They do the opposite of what is correct. It's sad to say, but no one was raised in a perfect home. All of us have issues to deal with, but some are more extreme than others.

We must grasp the principles of God's Word to bring a balance to how we raise our children. We want to raise our children in the nurture and admonition of the Lord. We desire to have our children grow up to be healthy and strong, with great marriages and children of their own. That's our dream and our goal, which should help motivate us to study the Word.

It's one thing to make a decision to be a biblical parent, but another thing to take the next step, which is action. There has to be action involved if you want to be a great parent. A good place to learn more about raising godly children is by reading the book of Proverbs. As you read, remember to think through the issues of your past when you were a child. Think about the challenges you are currently facing with your own children.

God has given us tremendous wisdom in the book of Proverbs on how to work with our children. Remember also what God tells us in James 1:5: *If any of you lacks wisdom, let him ask of God, who gives to all liberally and without reproach, and it will be given to him.*

Questions to Ponder

1. What is God's ideal family unit?

2. In thinking of your family's future generations, what decisions are you making today that are the same or different from your upbringing? What areas could use improvement?

3. What four questions can we ask in measuring ourselves as parents? Which one of these is a strength of yours?

Chapter 5
Examine Your Own Life

Recognize who you
are and be content
with who and what
you are.

I Love This Thing Called Parenting...

But let each one examine his own work, and then he will have rejoicing in himself alone, and not in another.

Galatians 6:4

Paul says to examine your own work, and then you will have rejoicing in yourself alone. In order to examine your own work, you need to know *your* strengths. Are you joyful with the work you are doing? Do you love to get up in the morning? Is there excitement about the challenges you get to conquer in your daily life?

Society today has become inundated with a victim mentality. There is a *poor me* mentality that many people live with and actually embrace. We love to talk about our problems, and we have sensationalized being *victimized*. We say, "I come from a dysfunctional family," and we highlight, honor, and make this statement valuable and important.

All of us are dysfunctional to some degree because we've all been raised by imperfect people. But do you want to stay in dysfunction, or do you want to learn and grow? Do you want to be stronger and become a great, powerful, happy, joyful, peaceful person? Personally, I want to be a happy, joyful, peaceful woman of God.

As parents, many of us are plagued with jealousies, insecurities, and inabilities. "I can't" is so strong within us that we become weak and ineffective. In a sense we allow our children to take control because we don't have the strength to be the leader in our home.

I was very young when I took on the parent role with my dad. I totally adored and loved my dad, but he was very weak at a point in his life and did not have the strength to lead our family. At that point our roles reversed.

Let's not be people who give away what God has

called us to be. When we give up and walk away from the role God has given us, it confuses things and makes the situation worse. It causes unhappiness and more problems.

Grow in Christ.

We need to become motivated to be strong people of God. We need to know who we are in Christ. We need to learn, grow, and gain confidence. We must decide to choose God's ways day by day, week by week, month by month, and year by year, and then we will see the changes that happen in our lives.

Many times we lack patience in our own personal growth. We want to see the changes right away. But be encouraged. It takes time to sow and to reap. You have to put the Word within you, and *then* it will begin to grow.

As parents, we must be secure or our teenagers will pull the carpet right out from under us. They are going to challenge what you believe, what you think you believe, and what you don't know that you believe. They are insecure but they will also push. If you don't have a sense of knowing who you are in Christ and have a security base within you, it can cause havoc in your home. If your children are younger, I encourage you to work on these issues in your life now.

Become Word-centered and become strong within yourself! Recognize who you are and be content with who and what you are. The Bible says to "rejoice in yourself alone" and not in another. If you have jealousy within you, it will be pulled out of you by the rejoicing in yourself. God's Word works!

Positive and negative influences.

There will always be people entering your children's lives of both positive and negative influence. It could be a teacher, youth pastor, or mentor. As a teenager, I remember a great woman who came into my life. Her name was Mary, and I ended up living with her family during my senior year of high school because my parents had moved. They allowed me to stay to graduate with the class I had gone to school with for several years. Mary was nice, warm, and a strong Christian. I was born again while living in this family's home, so my friendships and relationships began changing dramatically.

Mary was a stay-at-home mom with two children so I would have many opportunities to talk to her. I could tell my mom was jealous by the questions she would ask me. She would ask, "What are you talking to Mary about? Why can't you talk to me?" As a teenager I didn't have a strong relationship with my mom. It wasn't until I was in my thirties that we developed a healthy, good relationship. Now, I knew Mom didn't want to be jealous, but I remember thinking, *What is wrong with her? Why is she acting like this?* As I have gotten older, I recognize that she was insecure in her role as my mom – she didn't rejoice in herself alone, so when someone else came into my life, jealousy came into our relationship. If you are not strong in knowing who you are, when your child comes home and says, "Oh, I love being with this person. She is so funny and creative," you may feel insecure. If you are not strong in knowing who you are, when they start admiring qualities that you don't have, your insecurities will open the door to jealousy.

Parents, can I give you a bit of wisdom? Believe for people to come into your children's lives. Believe for other great godly men and women of all different ages and backgrounds who can input positively into your children's lives.

You must change things inside yourself to help your children grow up strong. I have always believed for significant godly men and women to serve as mentors to my children, but at the same time I establish the boundaries for the relationship. People who do not honor and love Jesus Christ as Lord and Savior will not mentor my children. I will not let a rebellious person have a significant voice into my children's lives. Children are always looking for people who will be influential in their lives. They like the older influence of grandparents, aunts and uncles, teachers, youth pastors, friends of the family – yet they may not always want *Mom* and *Dad*.

I encourage godly people to build relationships with my children. Those people who will speak positively into their lives, both male and female. I want to build those relationships, so I invite people of all ages into our home. Of course, being in church also encourages these relationships. You can usually find and trust certain teachers in Christian schools to be your children's mentors and models.

When my child comes home and says, "Oh, I love this and I love that about my teacher," I have to stay at the place that I can say, "I think that's great!" If any seed of jealousy starts to well up within me (because we are fleshly creatures), I stop the negative thoughts of, *this person would be a better parent. They probably like this person better than me.* Instead, I make myself think, *this person is helping my child to become stronger in the things of God.* Then I can rejoice in myself, and I can rejoice in the other godly people who are sowing great things into the hearts of my children.

Questions to Ponder

1. Why is it important to "examine yourself" in the area of parenting?

2. How do you think insecurity and jealousy affect your ability to parent?

3. How important is it for you to help your child build healthy relationships with other positive, influential adults?

Chapter 6
Fifteen Ways Parents Influence by Example

Trust God that what you are placing within your children will not return void.

We have to work hard as parents if we want to produce great kids. It's a sobering thought, but true. If we want to get good results, we have to do the work. I have put together fifteen simple guidelines for raising your children by your influence and example in their everyday lives. These are not in order of importance, but each one is vital to remember at different times of your day.

1. Keep your sense of humor.

Learn to laugh, play, joke, and have fun! When Casey feels stress in our home, he will start telling jokes or start food fights at the dinner table. The man is hysterical! Sometimes I am so serious and I think – *how can you do that?* I love the fact that Casey brings humor into our home and keeps things lighthearted instead of heavy and serious. Sometimes you literally have to do something that brings laughter into your home. Tease the children or play games with them. You set the tone of your home and keep potentially tense moments light by responding with humor rather than with anger and frustration.

2. Encourage and speak life into your children.

Plant seeds of life into your children by speaking God's Word over them daily. Look for the good in them and then tell what you see. Promote, talk about, and encourage them with positive, godly words. Don't only talk good about your children to other people; talk to *them* about the great things they are doing. Acknowledge their accomplishments. Be lavish with your encouragement and praise.

3. Pray for your children.

Speak the Word of God over your children as often and as much as you can. Find or write a confession to speak scripture into their lives. Pray for your children while you are driving or doing your dishes, grocery shopping, or taking a shower. In any part of your day when your children come to mind, speak the Word of God over them. Pray for them. Speak life into the relationships around them. I believe God for all of my children's friends, because every one of their friends has such a significant role in my child's development. When I was in kindergarten, one of my sisters developed a friendship with a little girl named Judy while in the third grade. Judy's family always yelled in their home. I never remember any yelling in my home until my sister started hanging around with Judy. Not only do I pray for my children, I pray for the children around them.

4. Touch and hug.

Touch in positive ways. Pat them on the head, on the back, or on their knee. When you are walking, take their hand if you can, depending on their age. The younger they are, the more you can hug and touch them. When you have little children, there is one very important word you need to know: *bonding*. If you spend the time bonding – snuggling, touching, and hugging – you will raise your children to be strong, healthy adults. There is nothing that communicates love better than physical touch!

5. Trust.

Trust, teach, and believe. Trust God that what you are placing within your children will not return void. Believe that when you are training them in the way of the Word, they are going to follow through in the way of the Word. Trust them. Believe in them. Believe that if everyone else goes the wrong way, your child will go the right way. There is something about your trust in your child that will produce someone who is worthy of that trust. Mistrust breeds disobedience, but when your children know without doubt that you trust them, it brings about a heart to do right.

6. Set boundaries.

We need to set boundaries for our children all the time and re-adjust them at every age and stage of growth. Be the *bad guy* when boundaries need to be set. Be the one who says, "No, that won't work." Teach your children they can't do something just because their friends are doing it, if it is not pleasing to God. If you need reassurance as a parent, talk to other like-minded parents who are raising their children to honor and love God. Casey and I often visit with other parents and ask, "What are you doing with your child at this age? What do you believe are the boundaries our children should have? How late should they stay out? Where should they go? What things should be a part of their life?" I don't always agree with every opinion, but I pray about it and ask God to show me what is right for our children and for our household. Be careful when setting your own boundaries that they are based on the Word, and not based on your own fear of what bad thing could happen. That is where great friends who know the Word will help bring balance to your thinking.

7. Know your own moral compass – the Word of God.

Know what you believe and why you believe it. We all have our moral compass on the inside that gives us direction in our lives. Be sure to talk about the Word with your kids. Talk about your morals – why you believe what you believe. Don't be a parent who says, "Because I said so!" Be the one who knows what you believe and are willing to teach your children the reasoning behind the decisions and directions you take as a family.

8. Pray *with* your children.

Don't let your children grow up without you praying *with* them. When our children were young we prayed with them every single day, whether it was in the car, or during other moments of the day, and we always prayed with them before they went to bed. We also pray as a family sometimes. The *family hour of prayer* is not our lifestyle of parenting, but on a regular basis Casey and I pray for and with our children. On a regular basis our whole family comes together and prays. We include any friends who are visiting to join in and pray with us. Prayer is a foundational part of who we are as people, and we want to make sure our children understand that, but also understand the how-to's of prayer. The best teacher is always your example!

9. Know your children's friends.

In addition to praying for your children's friends, you also want to *know* them. Talk with them. Find out who they are. Ask your child what they are like. Ask other kids, "How's so-and-so? What is he (or she) interested in?" Get to know the friends your children hang out with – be as much a part of their lives as you can. If you can, get to know their parents. That doesn't mean you need to be best friends with the parents of your child's friend, just know what basic beliefs they have and the standards they live by. Remember to communicate with the parents anything that is valuable to you. Make sure there is agreement.

10. Be there.

You cannot parent if you are not there. Several years ago, our daughter, Tasha, went to a sleepover with six other girls. The mother stayed up until 4:30 in the morning with them. I grumbled, *"Did she have to set that high of a standard for me?"* I would hate staying up until 4:30am! But when she did that I honestly thought (after the grumbling), *I love that.* This mother had four children and the youngest was my daughter's friend. All the children in this family were great examples of living strong for God. I thought, "That's a good example for me to follow." Tasha loved it. She said, "She stayed with us all night until 4:30, Mom." I said to Tasha, "I'll consider doing it. But maybe we just won't have a slumber party!" If your child has a sports game and you can't be there, talk about it with your child. My whole world does not revolve around my children, but my first plan of action is to support them and I am there when I   can be.

11.   Be in church.

Your children are going to follow your example. If you are not in church, they are not going to go to church. Your *example* of going to church will show your children the value you place on the teaching and training for life that only comes from being planted in the house of God. Your example will also help assimilate them into church life. I've heard people say, "We are at church all the time." I always want to ask them, "What does that mean, when you say you are there all the time?" Are you a Sunday morning saint or are you a *part* of your local church family; serving, helping, worshipping, learning the Word, and involved in what God is doing through the body of Christ?

12.   Talk, talk, talk with your children, and teach them to think.

I remember when my children were younger they would sometimes say, "That person is smoking. Boy, are they dumb!" I would say to them, "How do you know he is dumb?" There is a question that will make your child think. Instead of agreeing with the idea that smoking makes them a dumb person, we would talk about the choices people make. We would even talk about good people making dumb choices. Always ask your children questions and encourage them to think things through. You grow leaders that way. By encouraging them to think, you grow kids who are not going to walk out into the world and say, "I don't know what to do." It's so easy to make general statements about people and situations. It takes more time and effort to make your children think about what they are saying and why they believe it – but it's definitely worth it!

13. Vary your discipline methods.

Do not "idiot discipline" your children – meaning to do the same thing over and over! You should not say "you are grounded," for the fiftieth time in a row. They will be grounded all their life. They will hardly be able to wait to get out of your home. Be aware of what you are doing and why you are doing it. Make sure the discipline fits the situation and don't always just say and do the same things over and over. You have to take into consideration the bent of your child when using discipline. You have to take into consideration the time of their life, their age, and any other circumstances that possibly led to the behavior. Don't just do the same things without thinking about what you want your child to learn.

14. Increase your children's accountability and responsibility as they grow up.

Make a plan to give your children more and more responsibility. By the time they move out of your house, they should know how to do most of the basic tasks and chores they will need to live on their own. They should know how to balance their checkbook, how to clean, and the basics of cooking. They ought to know how to grocery shop, where to take the dry cleaning, and how to do anything they are going to need to do on their own. Teach them to be accountable for their life and for the responsibilities they begin to assume as they continue to mature.

15.   Love your husband/wife.

This may not seem like a parenting guideline, but it really is! Loving your husband, honoring him, and letting him know it will also spill over onto your children. Loving your wife by appreciating the gift God has given you will bring security to your home. Loving your wife by giving her gifts and flowers and taking her on special dates will show your children how to have a healthy marriage. They will see and appreciate the love and commitment you have with each other and it will bring security to their hearts and minds. The way you treat your spouse will give your sons and daughters a good role-model when the time comes to choose their own husband or wife. Your example as a couple who respects, honors, and loves one another will be the standard your children will expect in their own home.

Questions to Ponder

1. Which of the fifteen guidelines are currently strong areas of your parenting?

2. Identify three guidelines that need the most growth in your parenting. Then write out some specific changes you can make that will help you grow in each area.

3. Take a moment to speak some life words over your children and pray for them.

Part 2
Simple Wisdom For Raising Kids Who Love God!

Train up a child in the way he should go, and when he is old he will not depart from it.
Proverbs 22:6

Chapter 7
Guarding Your Most Precious Gift

If you make a conscious decision to guard your children,
it's amazing how dramatically your life will change.

I Love This Thing Called Parenting...

As parents, many times we concentrate on the outer appearance of our children so much that we are not alert to guard their inner man. You know what I mean, "You have the wrong socks on" or "You need to clean your face." Personally, I'd rather send my kid to school dirty-faced than dirty-hearted!

Most often parents have challenges with their teenagers because they weren't sensitive to guard their hearts when they were younger. We don't want to live in guilt because of it. Many have faced times when their teens won't even talk to them. When your teen turns away, won't talk to you, and shuts himself in his room for hours at a time, this is a serious indication to be on the alert.

I had a situation like this one with one of my children. At the time I thought, *I will not allow that kind of attitude.* So, I took his hand and said, "Come here, Honey. Momma wants to hug you." I embraced my child and his arms remained straight. I said, "I'm your Mom and I really love you. Now, if I talked sharply to you, I am sorry. But, it was a wrong way for you to act in that situation." I said, "I don't want you to get mean with Mom because that won't help you inside. It will make you sad inside." It took a little time and understanding, then we ended with a big hug. I didn't just walk away, but took the time to make sure we had broken down the barriers between us.
Don't let them build a wall.

Unfortunately, many times in the discipline of our children, we never go far enough with them, because we are not alert to the fact that we provoked anger in them. Then we walk away from the situation and leave it in a provoked state. Ultimately your child will love you and forgive you, but we may not realize that provoking them produced a little brick which is being used to build a brick wall between us and our child. This wall is being built little by little by little, one brick at a time.

I was in the sixth grade when I was hit by a car. This is an event that was hard to forget. At that point in my life I had already quit telling my mom that I loved her and I was not willing to hug her – *ever*. But when I was in the hospital and my mom walked in, I must have said, "I love you, Mom" fifty times! It was like a dam broke loose. I never said it again, though, until I was born again at the age of seventeen. My heart had been provoked and locked up. It took a major event, like the car accident, to open my heart up. Unfortunately, it quickly closed back up.

It is so easy for our children's hearts to close up and turn against us if we are not alert. We need to guard and protect them from a rebellious, stubborn attitude. Their flesh will rise up and the devil will use these opportunities to provoke and elevate the area that your child did not like. He will use that to make them think about it too. They are not too little to be drawn away by the evil one, so as parents we must be very wise in how we work with our kids, how we guard them, and how we protect them. We must be alert to the adverse one coming against them and not allow their emotions to close up and become hard against us.

Your words can build wedges between you and your children if are not sensitive and alert to their response. Many times they don't even consciously think of it. Your child doesn't consciously think, *Oh good, I'm building a wall against my parents.* But eventually they walk away from you. Their heart becomes cold to the relationship.

Slow down and guard your tone.

Be alert to how you are communicating with your children. That doesn't mean that you hover over, and are nervous about every word you say. It just means that you are smart and aware of any areas you may need to work on related to your speech. Don't be in such a hurry that you say things that hurt people. That's probably why God has really impressed me with the need *to guard*, because at times I have been very quick with my words.

In earlier years, Casey would sometimes say to me, "Do you realize how you just sounded?" He asked me many times, "Are you mad at that person? Are you mad at me? Are you mad at one of the kids?" I'd say, "No, I'm not mad at all." He would say, "Then you don't realize how you sounded when that came out of your mouth." Guard yourself and guard your kids!

Tips for Guarding

Here are some tips for guarding or protecting the spirit, soul, and body of your children. If you will consider these and put them into practice in your home you will see the difference in the attitudes of your children and enjoy a more fulfilling relationship with them.

1. Guard the words coming out of your mouth.

Psalm 141:3 says: *Set a guard, O Lord, over my mouth; keep watch over the door of my lips.* Some of us aren't used to thinking before we speak. We say whatever comes to mind without thought of the consequences. We need to tell ourselves repeatedly, "Set a guard over my mouth." Our tongues are not always quick to speak of the love of God and the blessing of the Lord. Too often it's the opposite.

To guard our family, we need to practice speaking life-giving words, and we need to have rooted within us the knowledge that life (and death) is spoken out of our mouths. To guard our family, we speak words of encouragement. We guard them with loving, uplifting words. We need to be quick to say, "Yes, I see you did that, and you did a good job."

When your children do something right it's easy to think, *well, they should be doing that.* Yes, they should be, but what's wrong with saying, "Good job of making your bed this morning. Good job of picking up your clothes. Man, I like the way you picked things up in the front room. You did a great job!"

What about your teenager? You could say to them, "Wow! You put your make-up on nicely this morning, Honey," or "Your hair looks so cool!"

Before a certain age my children had to ask my permission to turn on the TV. When our first son, Caleb, began to think he was old enough, he'd go in the room with the TV and turn it on. I would say, "I see you're watching something. I know that you make really good choices, right?" and he'd say, "Yes, Mom."

A second key to guarding our mouth is, "Call those things that are not as though they are." Show great trust for your children, and they will respond to that trust. I really work at teaching my children to make wise choices. I am their guard, yes, but I am not the one who is going to watch over them in all of the choices of their life. I've got to speak trusting words so they know how to make good choices when I am not with them.

How are kids supposed to know the best choice of

what to eat when they are small? As we were talking while eating dinner, I would say, "This is a good choice. This is why this is a good choice. This is why this is not the best choice, so if you choose this one, eat half of it." I would teach them to make wise choices.

You can teach them what is good to drink, not by harping at them but by guarding what you say. "This is what pop is made of, and this is what juice is made of." I always included water and mentioned its benefits because I wanted to teach my kids to drink water instead of all the other things. So I'd say, "If you are going to pick from these four things (as I set four things out), which is the best? Which is number one best? Number two best? Number three best? You guys make good choices."

Will they always make good choices? No, but they are going to get that *trustworthiness* as you speak it into them. When guarding your family, you have to watch what you say. Put a guard over your mouth.

2. Guard your steps, and the steps of your children.

As parents who want to raise children in the ways of God, there are choices we need to make regarding the places we go. One place we need to consider is how much time we will spend at the homes of relatives and extended family members. It's possible that some of our extended family will support our desire and be a part of helping train our children correctly for the Kingdom of God, but a lot of people do not have that same understanding. Many times our relatives are not in agreement with how we choose to raise our children.

If there is no agreement, why do we allow ungodly family members to be the baby-sitters of our children? Why do we place our most valued gift from God into the hands of people who will most likely not share our views on how we want to raise our children? They will allow and possibly even encourage them to do things that we don't want them involved with. Why do many people continuously put their children in an environment they can't trust? This is a very serious thought for us to consider: Why would we put our children in an environment that brought destruction to us? In order to really guard our children, we have to be brutally honest with ourselves.

On the positive side: Ask yourself a few questions about the places you *do* want to go. Many times we miss the opportunity to sow good seed into our children by planning really fun, memory-making activities with them. Our lack of fun activities makes what others are doing look tempting. Why not go swimming with your family? Why not go to the park? Or go and have a barbecue? Why not go mountain climbing?

Some women walk around with a depression cloud all around themselves. They don't do anything that is fresh and new. They don't develop new relationships or allow themselves to experience new environments. They're very closed in and let very few people into their lives.

I want to teach my children that we love people and we invite people into our home. We have a life full of fun. We have to make right choices and then do the necessary things to guard our family.

3. Guard what you watch.

With younger children, one of the biggest things I had to be careful of was the open preview weekends on cable TV. My kids were always so alert. It still bothers me that people pay to bring that garbage into their homes through TV.

There are great movies on some of the channels, but why not go to the library or to the video store and rent them? It will cost you less to rent them than to have cable because you don't watch it (you probably shouldn't watch it) all the time.

I was a TV addict as an older teenager. I would stay up until 2:00 or 3:00 in the morning watching TV, so I understand the lure of TV. You have to be very conscious of your own weakness and make sure that you guard against it in a wise way. And, if you have a lot of other interesting things going on in your life and you keep a really good attitude, your children will turn that TV off more and more.

4. Build friendships with great, godly people.

He who trusts in his own heart is a fool, but whoever walks wisely will be delivered (Proverbs 28:26). One of the great joys of pastoring the same church for over twenty-five years is the wonderful friendships we have built as a family. We have made it a priority in guarding our family by having great people around us. We have built great, godly, and strong friendships with people who give into our children's lives.

When my kids were small and wanted to go someplace with a friend I asked myself, *What kind of person is this – do they have the same godly values I have? How will this family protect and guard my child? What kind of parent are they?* It is so important to have these kinds of relationships surrounding you, with people you know and whom you trust with your most valuable treasure – people who really love your children. We can all tell when people really, truly love our children and will do their best to take care of them. Those are the people with whom we want to build long-term relationships.

5. Guard against bitterness and unforgiveness in your heart.

If *you* live in bitterness and unforgiveness, you will impart that spirit to your family. They will become angry people, walking around with an attitude, and they will have *a victim mentality*. People with bitterness, anger, and unforgiveness do not produce good fruit in their lives. When you have a heart full of pain and anger, you cannot raise children who are full of love and joy. It just does not work that way. When you are a "problem" person, everything is always falling apart, and everything is always a problem. Check yourself out. Are you mad at people? Are you unforgiving of people? If so, take some time to get with God and ask Him to forgive those who have wronged you and ask Him to forgive you also. You will be amazed how much your attitude and outlook on life will brighten.

6. Guard what you do and don't do.

Many times we do things we shouldn't and that gets us into trouble; but what about not doing the things we should be doing? When there is trouble in the family, do you skip church? When you are not feeling perfect, do you skip church? When you are irritated and someone at church hurt your feelings, do you skip church? Watch what you do...*and* what you don't do!

When my children were younger, they were like little guards over me. There were a couple of times that I said, "I am just going to stay home tonight." They would immediately say, "Why? What's going on, Mom? We don't stay home. Why do you want to do that, Mom?"

My kids saw me the day I got the phone call that my dad had died. Of course, I began crying right away. They were watching me. It was a Sunday night, but I stayed home from church that night with my mom. When the children came home from church, the first thing they said was, "Are you happy yet, Mom?" They were watching what I was doing. I said, "No, I am not happy yet, but I will be." The next morning my kids asked me, "Mom, are you happy now?" What they were really asking was, "What are you doing now?" Our children are watching us all the time.

If you and your husband argue and squabble, your kids will question, "What are you doing? What does this mean?" I don't think you should ever squabble in front of your kids, but I don't think you should never allow them to see any kind of conflict either.

Years ago Casey and I were in the midst of a discussion regarding an opposite point of view, when I noticed Caleb watching us. As we were bickering back and forth, I took the time to explain to Caleb, "By the way, Caleb, this is all right. I'm not mad at your dad." Casey added, "I'm not mad at your mom." Caleb said, "Okay." I told him, "We're not mad at each other, but we have different points of view and we are trying to figure out what we are going to agree on." "Oh, okay." Caleb continued doing what he was doing because he was at peace. He was okay with it.

Casey was around the age of twelve years old when he first heard his dad swear. Casey had thought a certain way about his dad up to that point, but he said right then he could remember thinking, "Oh, he's not a good guy."

Something clicked in him, and his opinion slightly changed at that point. That incident changed something on the inside of him. His dad influenced him in a negative way and probably never even realized it had happened.

When you are angry, what do you do? When you are irritated, what do you do? When you are frustrated, what do you do? When a storm of life is oppressing you, what do you do? When you can't get the bills paid, what do you do? How are you guarding your family? Are you alert to what you are saying and doing, or do you just let everything fly? How do you talk? This is very important in guarding your family.

It's amazing how you will think before you speak to your husband if you have a seven-year-old in your presence. Think about if Jesus was physically present and sitting in the room with you, what would you do? We have to challenge ourselves and really think through how we affect those we influence every day. If you will make a conscious decision to guard your children, it's amazing how dramatically your life will change.

Questions to Ponder

1. How can you work with your younger children to help prevent a hard heart when they become teenagers?

2. Review the six tips to guard the spirit, soul, and body of your children. Choose one area in which you are doing well, and give an example.

3. Choose one area from the six tips that you would like to improve and list specific goals you can set to help you improve in this area.

Chapter 8
Right Attitudes

There are some
basic attitudes
that must exist
in your home if
your children are
to be happy
and successful.

Be kind to one another, tenderhearted, forgiving one another, even as God in Christ forgave you.

Ephesians 4:32

There are some basic attitudes that must exist in your home if your children are to be happy and successful. God has so many great qualities that He would like to help us develop in order for us to be happy, successful people on this earth. The truth is *we* have to develop them! It would be nice if we were all perfectly kind, loving, forgiving, and thoughtful, but in reality we don't always do what we should. Sometimes we have attitudes that just aren't right, so we need to develop the right attitudes in ourselves and in our children.

Having the wrong attitudes can be a big thing, yet it's the small attitudes we deal with in our everyday life that can trip us up. Rather than tackling the big things like abuse, violence, neglect, and many of the other huge issues that often cause us to walk around with a "chip on our shoulder," I want to address the small issues that occur on a regular basis.

1. Have an attitude of forgiveness.

One of the small attitudes I want to address first is having an attitude of forgiveness. It could be that your husband is sometimes rude to you, or your kids aren't thoughtful. Maybe a friend forgot an appointment with you, or someone forgot your birthday.

These can seem like big things, yet they are very small in the scope of things that can happen in people's lives. The small thing that can destroy us is having an attitude of unforgiveness for those around us. If we don't live with an attitude that causes us to be quick to forgive and release the people involved, we will carry unforgiveness around with us. It will affect everything we do and it can infect the spirit of our home.

Sometimes we unknowingly say things that are very offensive to others, although we didn't intend to be rude or thoughtless. Have you ever blurted something out and realized later, "I can't believe I said that?" As a result, the person avoids us and we get offended, and think, *Don't they like me?*

Keep your foot out of your mouth!

Years ago we were at a dinner party. The host brought up the topic of radar detectors. I began talking about how wrong it is to use them because obviously your intent is to break the law by speeding. As I went on and on, suddenly the host asked another couple, "Do you have one?" Of course they said, "Yes!" I thought, *why did she have to ask them with me going on and on about it?* Even though I wasn't the only one who had rattled on, I thought, *I can't believe it. I totally stuck my foot in my mouth.* I have found that when you talk a lot, you tend to get your foot stuck in your mouth a lot. That's just the way it goes.

It's a fact of life that people can say things that are innocent to them, yet someone else can easily become offended. We have all done it. We need to be quick to believe others aren't trying to offend us on purpose, and we need to forgive ourselves when we are the ones sticking our foot in our mouths. For instance, I had to forgive myself for being so verbal in the conversation about radar detectors. Later, I went to the man who had the radar detector and said, "I'm really sorry. It's just an opinion. If you want to have one, that's your business. I'm not telling you that you are in sin from a pastoral point of view." Then he told me,

"I threw it away," and continued to tell me that he had never thought about it that way before. I said, "Oh, good!" but I had to forgive myself for being too quick to speak and I'm pretty sure he probably had to forgive me, too! From then on, I determined to ask a few more questions before I voice my opinion! Remember Romans 12:3, which tells us not to think too highly of ourselves!

If you want to have an attitude of joy, peace, and happiness in your life, you have to learn to have an attitude of forgiveness. Many times we are offended by our family, our relatives, or our friends, not because they purposely tried to hurt us, but because they innocently hurt us. They didn't intentionally hurt us, so let's recognize that people make mistakes and instead of carrying all of our feelings at the ends of our fingertips, learn how to forgive. Don't take everything as a personal attack. Let it go and forgive. **Forgiveness goes both ways.**

Ask for forgiveness when you need to be forgiven. But, let me just say this, don't ever ask a person to forgive you for your unspoken thoughts. You can talk to God and get things right, but don't put those bad feelings on another person. Ask forgiveness for your *actions* – what you did against another person – not for your *thoughts*.

There were a few times when my children were very young that I'd get very frustrated with them. They would do things wrong and I would think, *I can't believe it; just obey me!* Sometimes they would just do their own thing! One evening we had friends over for a big dinner at our house. Our dinner rule was if you ate all your dinner, you could have dessert. All of the adults ate their meal and got dessert. The kids didn't eat all of their meal so they didn't get dessert. That meant instead of enjoying my guests, I was dealing with their frustration about not having any dessert. In the midst of my frustration I took Caleb's little arm and I grabbed it. It was an act of total frustration. It had nothing to do with discipline. It had nothing to do with loving him. It had nothing to do with training or teaching him in the way that he should go. It had everything to do with *my frustration* of not being able to handle the situation. It wasn't his fault; it was my fault.

When we get frustrated with our kids, it's really not our kids' fault. It's our own fault. I'm not trying to point an accusing finger at us, but in most cases we either let the situation go too far or we have other things we are dealing with.

When I grabbed Caleb's arm, he was surprised that I did that. I said, "I'm so sorry, Son. I got frustrated with you. I got frustrated with the way you were behaving and that's my fault. I am sorry."

There is nothing wrong with saying you are sorry to your kids. In fact, you can teach your kids tremendous things by saying, "I'm sorry," and admitting that you are wrong. They already know you are wrong. They knew that when you reacted to them. So I said, "I'm sorry, Son. Mom's just really sorry. Let's start this over again."

I had to correct their behavior, because the way they were acting wasn't right, but I also wanted to teach my kids that they have to ask for forgiveness when they do wrong things. The best teacher is always by example. If we want our children to do what we say, we have to be willing to live by the same guidelines.

2. Have an attitude of kindness.

Speak lovingly in your home. Proverbs 16:24 says: **Pleasant words are like a honeycomb, sweetness to the soul** *and health to the bones.* Proverbs 15:1 says: *A soft answer turns away wrath, but a harsh word stirs up anger.* Speak thoughtfully and kindly in your home. Speak with consideration. Think about what you are saying and to whom you are saying it to. It seems we can sometimes be the most unkind and rude to our family members.

In learning how to speak with love, a good place to start is your *tone of voice.* Several years ago we had a panel of ladies answering questions from the audience. One young mother stood up and asked (in a very whiney voice), "I've been trying to teach my child how to quit whining, and I just can't get him to quit." You could hear it in her voice. She didn't realize that she was whining. It was a blind spot to her, but we could all hear that whiney tone.

I can have a very direct type of tone when I talk to people. I have had people respond to me as if they thought I was demanding something of them. I thought, *I didn't mean it like that. I meant, "Would you like to?" Not, "Go do it."* I certainly don't have a whiney tone, but I can command. That's the thing I have to really work on so that when I speak people perceive me correctly. As I became aware of this issue I made a decision to change it. On purpose I would catch myself in mid-sentence as I was speaking tough and I would make the effort to change it.

Early in our marriage I would tell Casey what to do. I would say, "Hurry up. Go do this and this and this." He would say, "Yes, ma'am." He did it on purpose to totally irritate me. But, it was a good lesson for me and it helped me become aware of how I was speaking.

Are we speaking in love? Are we using soft, edifying, pleasant words, or are we harsh, commanding, boring, or without energy? When Tasha was a small child and she became whiney, I'd pick her up and dance around, sing her a song, and tell her she could talk nice. Sometimes she would get spanked for whining, have to stand in the corner, or be sent to her room. Train your children not to be whiney, but train yourself too.

Sometimes I would catch myself and I'd say, "Mommy's going to stand in the corner." My kids would chase me into the corner! I'd ask, "Can I come out?" "No, Mom." Even when disciplining your children, you can keep an attitude of love. Your home can be happy and fun.

3. Have an attitude of responsibility.

Have an attitude to teach and train your children to assume responsibility. Years ago I was working with some young people and I realized that they didn't know how to do the most basic tasks. They were old enough to have known what to do in the kitchen, how to clean the bathroom, and how to do their own laundry. I thought, *why haven't their parents taught them what to do in the kitchen? Why haven't they trained their children?* I'm talking about basic, simple things.

I looked at this one young person and I thought, *she can't even peel a potato.* Then I thought, *whose fault is it?* It's the parents' responsibility to train and teach their children. It really made me question, *are we training and teaching our children in the basics of life?*

We have to teach responsibility.

We must have an attitude of teaching our children – male and female – all kinds of basic responsibilities. Teach and train your boys (as well as your girls), how to vacuum and make their beds. Our children have to acquire an attitude to learn. They will need to know how to take care of the basic tasks in life and it does not help them in the long run if we do everything for them.

A nine or ten-year-old could be responsible for preparing one meal a week. But, you can't expect your child to prepare a meal if you haven't trained them from an early age how to do the basics: cut the vegetables, make a salad, make a meatloaf, or even how to properly stir something on the stove and not burn the food or themselves. I know it's a lot harder to teach and train them than it is for you to do it yourself, but that's how they learn.

Teach them how to sort laundry. I didn't know how to sort laundry when I got married. With six kids, my mom just did it all herself. She put the clothes away, washed windows, dusted, cleaned bathrooms, and washed the car.

One summer I looked after two young children every Wednesday. They wanted to wash the car. You'd better know it was still dirty after they got done, but they had to practice to learn how to do it. I also had them working in the flowers, removing the dead leaves and cleaning them up. Yes, they pulled out some of my good flowers. That's what they do when they are learning. Your kids have to learn how to be responsible in the home, and you have to teach and train them in all the different areas.

Make sure your second and third child learn responsibilities as well as the oldest child. When the kids were small, Caleb would sometimes make Tasha's and Micah's bed. Caleb would say, "Oh, I'll make your bed for you," and he would make it. I would let him make the bed once in a while, but not all the time because then they wouldn't learn to do it themselves. We also had to make sure Micah, our youngest, wouldn't suffer from the baby syndrome – with everything done for him.

Train your children how to do basic *in-the-home* skills and *outside-the-home* skills. When they are old enough, train them how to balance a checkbook and how to use a credit card. Teach them how to change a tire and check the oil in their car. There are so many simple things we can help our children learn at the appropriate time that will save them heartache, frustration, and embarrassment in the long run.

II Thessalonians 3:10 says: *If anyone will not work, neither shall he eat.* This means our attitude must be that the whole family is involved in the work of running our households. Every family member needs to be a part of taking care of the house, not just the "momma" doing it all.

4. Have an attitude of peace.

You need time alone with the Lord – just you and God. Mark 6:46 says: *And when He had sent them away, He departed to the mountain to pray.*

Your schedule may be so packed that there is not any time for you to just be alone. You have no thought time to reflect or think quietly or time of non-responsibility where you don't have to do anything; you don't have to spank anyone; you don't have to help with homework; you don't have to drive someone to a soccer game or pick them up from cheer practice.

I truly believe that godly friends are an extremely important part of our overall emotional health, but sometimes friends can infringe on the time you need to spend alone. You need to plan for time to relax your mind and relax from all the activities going on around you. You need your own personal growth time. Just like Jesus sent all of the disciples and the multitudes away so He could be alone, we need to have time to get away. Jesus also prayed, and that is very important. But, you also need to have that time where you can relax or just sit down and have some coffee or enjoy a cup of tea.

I have an aunt who takes an afternoon break with a cup of coffee and one miniature Snickers bar. Every single day she relaxes for about an hour, regroups, and gets herself together. She has raised four successful children, she has grandchildren who are living for God, and she is a very healthy, happy woman.

When my children were young, my time alone was during their naptime. During that season, Casey rode his bicycle on Saturdays with a bunch of his guy friends, so Saturday afternoons were my alone-time, too. Then several of the people riding with him began coming over to the house and staying to visit. It started to bother me that they were there and I would want them to leave. Finally I figured out why I was upset every week and I told Casey, "I realize why I'm so resentful of everyone coming over; it's because they are infringing on my alone time." During that time I always turned off my phone and didn't answer the door because I wanted to use that time to be refreshed for my family. It is a necessity to do that for yourself if you want to have peace in your life.

If someone starts infringing on your time, be bold and courageous enough to say, "This is my time." We need to value and protect this time. Like Jesus said, "I'm going up to the mountain right now to pray." If you start giving up that time because you are drawn away by activities, friends, or family needs, whether they are fun and exciting or not, you will begin to grow weary. We need to take the time to refresh ourselves so we can be the powerful parents God wants us to be.

Questions to Ponder

1. Are you scheduling alone-time for yourself on a regular basis? If not, write down ideas for how you can make this work for you.

2. List a few responsibilities that you feel are important to train your children to accomplish. Come up with one new activity that will help you train your children in these responsibilities.

3. Are there people or tasks that seem to regularly infringe on your time alone? What can you do this week to make a change in this area?

Chapter 9
Filling Their Tanks

As influential parents, we are to walk as Christ walked and love as He loved, even when our children are the most unlovable.

The wise woman builds her house, but the foolish pulls it down with her hands.

Proverbs 14:1

In John 3:16 Jesus said: *For God so loved the world that He gave His only begotten Son, that whoever believes in Him should not perish but have everlasting life.* God so loved you and me that He gave.

Romans 5:8 says: *But God demonstrates His own love toward us, in that while we were still sinners, Christ died for us.* While we were still sinners Christ died for you and me. This shows the bigness of God's love. He loved us when we were yucky, mean, rude, crude, nasty, thoughtless, unforgiving, bratty, inconsiderate, snotty, vengeful, and rebellious. In our worst state, Jesus loved us.
God gave Jesus for us.

God so loved that He gave His only begotten Son so we could be saved. Think of that! Now we are to walk on this earth as examples of Jesus. He is our example for how we are to walk. As He is, so are we in this world. So we are to walk as He walked, and He walked in love.

Jesus loved the ones who cried out, "Crucify Him!" as much as He loves us. His love hasn't changed no matter how evil and wicked a person has been, including Hitler. Hitler didn't respond to that love, but God still loved him the same as anyone else. As influential parents, we are to walk as Christ walked and love as He loved, even when our children are the most unlovable. We can be that loving factor in our home if we will allow the Spirit of God to work in us.

I believe metaphorically there's a little "invisible" tank inside of every person that affects our emotional wellbeing. Like a gas tank, it requires regular filling. If our emotional tank is not filled up on a regular basis it can become empty or low. Our tanks need to be filled with God's love regularly. Every person's tank can hit low or empty, including the tanks of our children. As great parents, we need to know how to fill up their emotional tanks.

Here are a few "refueling" guidelines to help keep our children running on a full tank:

Unconditional acceptance.

Unconditional acceptance is one way to refill someone's emotional tank.

Have you ever noticed how you think your own children are perfect, while other people's children are not? When my children were ages four, two, and a few months old a little girl stayed at our house for a week. For the first four days I thought she was totally responsible for all the bad behavior that was happening in our home. I thought, *if you would stop treating my son that way, he wouldn't do that kind of stuff.* By about the fourth day, I figured out that it wasn't totally her fault. My children were a part of the problem, too! After realizing that, I was able to discipline all of the kids better because the first few days I was consumed with, "my kid is right and yours is wrong." I had an *unconditional acceptance* of my children.

It is a very positive quality for us, as parents, to have *unconditional acceptance* towards our children, even when they do wrong. Now, that doesn't mean that we don't discipline. You may have older children who are rebellious. Even if they aren't saved, you have to look beyond their actions and love them unconditionally, no matter what they do.

When Caleb was small, (I don't know if it was

because he was the firstborn and a perfectionist) he always wanted the first place in our family, even over Casey. I remember one time Casey brought me a rose. I said to Caleb, "Look, your daddy brought me a rose." He said, "No, Mommy, I got that for you, but Daddy pushed me out of the way and he gave it to you instead."

If I had not understood and taken the time to deal with it, that could have been a real weakness in Caleb's growth and development. I thought, *man, if he were older, that could really be a very insecure statement, like, "No, no, no, I'm important too!"* As mothers we have to be wise. So, I put my arm around Caleb and I said, "Sweetheart, you know what? Whether you give me anything or not, you are just wonderful."

Think of ways you can express unconditional acceptance to the people who are around you – your husband, your children, and of course, your friends. Possibly your teenagers are going through a tremendous challenge in school, and they are not getting the kind of grades that they want to have and that you want them to have. You could say something like, "You know, Sweetheart, grades aren't going to make or break you. You have the capabilities to do tremendous things. You are important, and I believe in you. I know you will do your best."

As parents, we sometimes get so concerned with their grades. Encourage diligence in schoolwork, but don't forget as you love and value your children you are keeping their emotional tanks full.

Affection.

The second quality to remember in filling the tank of

your children is *affection* – hugging, kissing, loving, and touching.

As babies, I held my children and kissed them; I spoke into their faces, and told them how much I loved them. Then, as they grew, my kids were constantly coming to me to get hugs and snuggles! I would say, "Come on, let's get snuggles." Or, Tasha would say, "I want to snuggle." She would go get her blanket and pillow and put her pillow on my lap. Then she would snuggle right in.

I trained my children to be affectionate. Some people would say – *my kids really aren't huggers.* I would have to say, "Really?" I honestly believe we train them that way! As your children begin to grow up, some of them won't let you kiss and hug them because you didn't *train* them that way. When you talk to them, put your hand on their shoulders or touch them. Your touch will transmit affection.

If your child comes to tell you something and you are busy doing something, have you ever considered stopping what you are doing and looking at them? Just look at them, and give them your full attention. As we place that much value on our child, we will help fill their tank.

If they are watching TV, just sit down in a chair, look at them and smile. They will look at you and ask, "What are you doing?" You can respond, "You know something? You are so cool." Or, you may say, "Do you know how good-looking you are?" They may respond with an, "Oh, Mom!" We have to go ahead and say it anyway. Say words of encouragement to them, touch, hug, kiss, and tickle them. I've heard it said that every person needs at least seven hugs a day.

I heard of a study done several years ago that

indicated boys received one-sixth of the physical affection – the hugs, pats, and love – that the girls received. Another interesting fact was, in first grade the boys were in six times the amount of fights as the girls. As our boys grow older, many of us mothers don't think about their need for hugs and affection. Yet inside, their emotional tanks are still saying, "Please touch me." We can touch our sons in a loving way and work on filling their tank, with just a simple pat, hug, or kiss on the cheek. Instead of just saying, "Hi," walk by your son and say, "Boy, are you looking good!"

You can also make life humorous and fun along with touching them. When your kids walk in the door you can say, "Wow! You look good! I'm so glad you're home." A gentle touch or a little teasing can help break down walls that have been built up within teenagers. Micah, our youngest son, is very strong in the area of physical touch. That is his "love language" and I make sure that his cup is full. As parents we have to take responsibility to hug and touch our kids.

When my kids were younger, I would always sit down with them in the morning. They would come and sit in my lap and we would just sit there for five, ten, fifteen, or twenty minutes, where they received my total attention. Often the time would vary, but I was filling up their tanks. If they are having problems, it may be that their tanks aren't full. Even in an otherwise healthy home environment, sometimes I believe young girls who end up pregnant are looking for the love and acceptance that comes from positive physical touch.

As moms, we are the ones who need to really be aware of filling their emotional tanks. Maybe you can get up a few minutes earlier and sit on your child's bed. Talk

lovingly to them as they are waking up. Even when teenagers act as if they don't want hugged, as parents we need to do it anyway (not, however, in front of their friends to embarrass them). The principle of Luke 6:38a works: *Give and it will be given to you.*
Approval.

The third quality to remember in filling the tanks of your children is *approval*. Notice the good things – the positive things – your children are doing, not the horrible, negative things. Listen for your children to say a thoughtful word to each other. Later, when you are alone with the one who said the good words (maybe when you are driving somewhere in the car) you can say, "You know something, Sweetheart? I noticed how nicely you were talking to your sister, and you really are thoughtful." When you have the chance to compliment them on something good, don't let the opportunity pass you by!

When your kids do something in a sports game, you can't run out onto the field and give them a high five, but later you can say, "Wow! You did a great job!" Maybe you don't even tell them that day, but two or three days later, you say, "You know something? I watched you on the field a couple days ago. I'm so proud of you. You treated everyone with such thoughtfulness." Now, maybe in another game they were beating up on each other, but *notice the good and encourage the good.*
Notice the good.

When your children bring you a school paper with five things wrong and five things right, don't look at the five things wrong. Look at the five things that are right. It helps to build them up when you show approval for what they have done that's right.

We need to outwardly notice when the people in your life do something well. When you pick your children up from their caregiver or from the daycare where they are being watched, express appreciation and approval. "I really appreciate you being with my children today." Fill the tanks of others every chance you get and it will come back to you!

Questions to Ponder

1. Write down the three major ways to fill up your children's "tank."

2. In your childhood, which of these were used in your household? Which were not?

3. Write one new goal for improving the way you fill your children's tank.

Chapter 10
Ten to One

Every day think of ten good things for every child for each time you might have to discipline.

Many times it is the simple things that bring great success into our lives. I heard something many years ago that I thought was one of the best parenting tools I've ever heard. And this is it: notice *ten positive* things about your child to every *one* thing that is wrong or negative. You have to discipline, but look for ten things you don't have to discipline for to the one that you do.

In looking for the good in our children we have to be very aware and smart. Now if I look for the same characteristics with which to praise Tasha as I see in Caleb or Micah, I'm going to miss it. You have to look for the individuality of each child.

In looking for the good in your child, if you think, *man, I hope my child does this*, because you saw your other child do it, and he doesn't do it, don't say anything to your child. Each child is different from any other, so don't compare one child to another. Your child is motivated by a different gifting; he has a different personality, and a different calling than any other child.

There are certain characteristics about my children that are really good. I don't need to focus on what I see other children do that mine don't. I can see those things because I'm not blind (and my kids are not perfect), but I want to focus on the really great things about them. Focus on the good things in your children and look for what is wonderful.

Many times we get so consumed with what we want instead of looking for good things all around us. Let's look for the positives in life, whether it is in your spouse, your children, a roommate, or someone else.

If the wise woman builds her house as Proverbs 14:1

says, what do you want as your foundation? Do you want praise, love, affection, adoration, approval, and acceptance, or do you want to always think, *I'm mad at you, I don't like this house, I have to get out of here,* because life just does not live up to your expectations.

Every day think of ten good things for every child for each time you might have to discipline. So, deal with the one negative issue, but think of ten wonderful things too; then the one negative will seem very, very insignificant. It will not blow up into a huge problem.

Positive actions are a great reward.

Positive actions aren't just giving a candy bar to reward your child. Positive actions come through love, touching, a smile, a pat on the head, a big hug, and a kiss. It also comes through the rewards of other things. It may be in giving back the toy they lost earlier because of disobedience. Maybe they do get something sweet that they wanted. Positively reinforce quick obedience. It could be as simple as saying, "Man, you are the most obedient child. You are a joy in my house."

I remember one day when Caleb was small. We had some people over and he was just running, running, running around and having the best time. As he ran by me I leaned down, got right in his face, and kissed him very fast, then he proceeded to run. After about five minutes he came to me and asked, "Why did you kiss me?"

I answered, "Do you know why? Because you're just so cool! You are so fun to have around because you are having so much fun. I enjoy just watching you." He said, "Oh," and off he went. It was just a small thing, but he gave me an opportunity to reinforce positive behavior in him.

There may be challenges every day with your children, dealing with the different personalities, and knowing what to do. We have to pray in the Spirit over the numerous situations that come up. Sometimes we don't handle a situation in the best way because of our own insecurities and our own questions.

I Peter 4:8b says: *love will cover a multitude of sins.* Sin is just missing the mark. As parents we do miss the mark. We are not perfect moms and we're not super dads.

I look back over my life and think, *I was a good kid,* yet I can remember stealing in kindergarten. My parents didn't teach me to steal. They never stole anything, because that was not a part of their lifestyle. My dad never smoked in his whole life, but I did as a young girl. Can you believe it? I lied, but my parents didn't teach me to lie.

We went to church, and Mom and Dad did what they knew to do. They didn't teach me to do wrong things. They prayed for us diligently. They believed God that all six of us kids would grow up to be strong in the Lord, but we still did imperfect things. With our children, we must walk by faith and not by sight, because sometimes our children can look like perfect little angels, but in their hearts they are not angels at all!

Don't be so quick to judge.

Sometimes we judge so quickly concerning our children that we don't let the long-term effects of the love, training, and commitment on our part reap a harvest in them. We are not going to be perfect, and we're not going to do everything right. But as we continually sow encouragement and reinforce the great things we see in our children, they will be drawn into being who we say that they are.

In our marriages, we're not super wives and we're not going to do everything right. We blow up when we shouldn't and we say words that we shouldn't. We act idiotic at times, jealous, insecure, and greedy. When an offering is taken and your husband wants to put in a big check, inside yourself you say, "No," then you feel guilty for not wanting to give. We put such pressure on ourselves sometimes to perform to these great expectations. We feel like we can't tell anyone how we feel because they are "perfect." That's a lie that the devil would love for us to believe.

The devil loves for you to be all alone in your thoughts, to think negative and evil of yourself. He likes you to believe you are the only one who thinks that way. That kind of thinking will keep you feeling bad about yourself, so just decide, "I'm not *Super-mom*. I'm not *Super-wife*. I'm not *Super-friend*."

Friendship was something that really challenged me once I had children. Because of the change in my priorities and to my schedule I had the thought; *I'm not a great friend anymore*. I really had to think about this new phase of my life. After much thought and prayer I decided, "Wait a minute. My friendships are lasting relationships that can survive the seasons of life. That *is* being a great friend." Time-wise it may not be the same right now, but many times the friendship didn't have to change. A true friend will recognize the different seasons of our lives and be willing to make adjustments in your relationship. We have to change our thinking to be content rather than miserable and feeling guilty all the time.

Changing with the seasons of life.

It's crucial to stay on top of using the ten to one rule, especially when we don't feel like it. That's the time we really need to concentrate and watch for opportunities to say something positive to our children. I've had people say to me, "Well, have you ever been around my kid? Do you know how hard it is to find something good about them?" I've had to deal with parents whose children live with an ex-mate or with someone else. Many felt like, "We don't have the influence on them all the time, so when we do get them for a very brief time, it's almost like, *glory to God*, when the two weeks are over."

I have responded, "Now wait a minute. There is something in every person that is positive." It could be as simple as, "You have the prettiest long eyelashes." "You look great." "I like that color on you." Sometimes we try to think of something that's huge instead of the simple things.

It could be as simple as your children are watching a TV program and it is a good choice. I mean, out of all the things they could have watched, they picked the best. Tell your children, "That was a good selection." Say something positive about what they are doing. Work diligently on saying positive things to your children because a child will rise to what you believe and say about him or her.

When a person comes up to you and says something like, "What a beautiful blouse," does that influence how many times you want to wear that blouse? You probably want to wear it more! When twelve people tell you how wonderful you look in a certain outfit, it's really easy to wear it five more times in the same week.

Our children respond to this same principle. You

could say in faith to your child, "You know, the righteousness of Christ is all over you." If you say that to a thirteen-year-old and they don't know God (you are saved but they aren't), they might say, "I can't believe it, Mom. Don't talk like that."

Teach siblings to love one another.

When my children were small, every time Micah kissed his sister, I'd say, "Oh, what a great little brother you are. You are so good." When I was pregnant with Micah and Caleb would do something for Tasha, I would say, "Because you are such a good big brother, we want to have another baby for you to be a big brother to." Tasha wasn't as outgoing in expressing love to her big brother, so I had to encourage her. "Tasha, you have such a loving big brother. You are such a loving little sister. You are so blessed." Every time I saw something, I would speak it into them. I would say that they love to be with each other and they are all kind-hearted to each other.

I didn't want to have teenagers who battle it out. I wanted them to recognize that they can be best buddies, and grow up to trust each other. And now that they are older, I see the fruit of this principle working in them. They truly love each other, encourage each other, and are extremely strong supporters of each other. I am amazed at the strength of the love and commitment between all of our kids.

My big brother was two years older than me, but I didn't recognize that I could use him as a resource to say, "John, what do I do?" I never knew I could look to him as a friend. I only knew he was my big brother, and I was always kind of afraid of him. So I told my children consistently when they were small, "You are best buddies" and "Mommy is your best buddy. Dad is your best buddy." Speak words of faith into your family of what you want to see.

Do not compare your children.

Another key is, don't compare your children to each other. Be very careful that you don't compare your children. Each is very different, so if you are giving positive affirmation to all of your children in the same way, you could be in trouble. This is especially true if your first child is aggressive and quick to do everything. Be very sensitive not to demand that of your second and third child.

Caleb walked when he was ten-and-a-half months old. Tasha walked when she was about fifteen-and-a-half months old, and Micah took a little longer. They were all different. I was so glad that I had a number of people talk to me about their children walking at different ages so that I didn't put unrealistic expectations on Tasha or Micah.

I thought, *as much as Tasha slept in her first couple of months, she's not going to walk real fast, because she doesn't want to.* It was true. It didn't bother me, but it could have if I had been thinking, *what are you doing? Your brother walked at ten-and-a-half months.* Some people said, "Doesn't she walk yet?" I just answered, "No, she will when she's ready." And when the same thing happened with Micah, I was prepared.

Some children in the same family are skinny while others are heavier. Their metabolism is different. God created us as *individuals*, but we try to put everyone in the same little box. In giving positive affirmation, you have to look at your children individually and be very careful of the words you speak.

Questions to Ponder

1. What are some of the good qualities you see in your child you can reinforce?

2. Take a minute to consider any ways you compare your child to their siblings or their friends. Write down a couple ways you can promote the differences rather than compare.

3. Look up and write down two scriptures you can confess over your child this week.

Chapter 11
When Push Comes To Shove

As we lead and guide our children into right choices, they have the freedom to see their choice, understand the choice, and make it based on their will.

The Lord is my shepherd; I shall not want. He makes me lie down in green pastures; He leads me beside the still waters. He restores my soul; He leads me in the paths of righteousness...

Psalm 23:1-3

It is evident from these verses in Psalm 23 that God *leads* us. He does not *push* us! He doesn't push us into making choices in life; rather He *leads* us into making proper choices. The next key to raising great children is called the "string principle" which is simply pulling your children (or leading them), instead of pushing them.

You know how easy it is to pull a string. You pull it in the direction you want it to go and it simply follows along. How about trying to push a string? When you try to *push* that same string, it ends up in a big messy pile.

This principle works the same way with our children. As we lead and guide them into right choices, they have the freedom to see their choice, understand the choice, and make it based on their will. When we try to push our kids into making the choices we want them to, it can become a big fight. No one wants to be pushed and told what to do all the time.

Here are a few guidelines that will help you operate in the string principle:

1. Observe your child's personality.

Who is this child God has placed in your home? Is your child easygoing, a mediator, or a leader? What type of personality does she or he have? In understanding your child's personality and after deciding to use the principle of pulling instead of pushing, you could say, "In five minutes

Mommy wants you to come and do something. You need to start to put these things away now, Sweetheart."

Then, because you are aware of his personality style, you might say in two minutes, "You have three more minutes," You are being wise in dealing with him instead of just demanding your own way. You need to learn your child's ways and understand his bent, not just push him into a corner all the time.

When Tasha was small, one day she suddenly reacted to a situation in a different way than she normally had reacted. From that day forward she had changed. Something had changed in her and I knew it. I had to learn to work with her differently than I had the day before. So you have to watch what is happening with your kids because they are growing and changing every day.

2. Talk to your child about what is happening.

Talk to your children instead of demanding from them. Take the time to prepare them for change. Be careful not to always interrupt them. If you want to lead rather than push, you need to be considerate of the things they are involved with and not just have them quickly stop what they are interested in doing.

When Caleb was little, the hardest time of the day was right before bedtime when he was playing with Casey. I solved the problem by saying, "Caleb, you get to play with Daddy twenty more minutes, then bedtime." He would say, "Okay, Mom." At ten minutes I'd say, "You get ten more minutes to play with Dad, and then it's bedtime." Then I counted down the minutes.

I would say, "One minute, Caleb." Then I'd say, "Caleb, do you want Mommy to put you to bed or do you want Daddy to put you to bed?" I already knew his answer, but I wanted him to be led instead of me pushing him. He would say, "I want Daddy." I said, "Okay, come give Mom a kiss." So we'd kiss and hug and I'd tickle him. I said, "See you later." Off to bed he'd go. When I forgot to do that, we'd have a battle at bedtime because there was no preparation.

3. Ask, don't demand – allow your children to make choices.

Ask instead of always demanding from your children to do what you want them to do. When possible, give your child a choice. "Do you want this, or do you want that?" I have worked at always giving my children choices.

There was a family Casey and I observed long before we had kids of our own. Their children were always happy and very obedient. I mean, the parents would say "boo" to them and they would say, "Do you need something?" They appeared to be very contented children, so we decided to talk to the parents to learn their secret. We asked them, "Why are your kids so content and happy? Tell us some of the things you do with your kids." The father said, "For one thing, usually we give our children choices instead of demanding from them what we want them to do."

As an example, when your child wants something to do, you could say, "You can play in the house with your blocks and with your cars, or you can read some stories. We can bake some cookies, or you can go to Timmy's house for an hour and play with him. Now what would you like to do?" Give them a choice.

If I had several leftovers in the refrigerator – I would ask, "Micah, would you like roast beef or spaghetti for lunch?" I could have chosen for him, but why do that when I can teach him to choose?

I can hear some mothers say, "But you don't have four kids to feed for lunch." I had three and I let them all choose. Most of us have microwaves. Get your Tupperware out, fill it, and put it in the microwave, then put the leftovers back in the refrigerator. It's not that hard to give choices.

You know how kids fight over sitting in the car? Give them choices at times. When Caleb was little, he would sometimes want to sit by his sister, or brother, or sit in the backseat, or sit in the front seat with me. He always liked to go with his dad, but sometimes he didn't have that choice.

Teach your children how to make choices. Responsible people know how to make choices and how to make them quickly. It's all the process of teaching them how to make choices. It is sad how many people just can't make a decision...about anything! Most likely their parents didn't give them an opportunity when they were young to make choices of their own, so they grew into adults who are afraid and don't know how to choose. They can't figure out if they want the blue shoes or the black shoes.

God made each of us with a free will and He gives us the ability to make choices every day. He leads and guides us, but never pushes. As great parents, let's do the same for our kids that God does for His!

Questions to Ponder

1. In what ways do you "push" rather than lead your child?

2. Do you take the time to prepare your child for change or do you demand they instantly obey you?

3. How can you better lead your child and allow them to begin making choices that are appropriate for their age? Write down specific areas you will begin to allow them to make choices.

Chapter 12
Saying "Yes" Instead of "No"

If we are willing to work and take the time to think about
our response to our children, we can turn things around
so we are saying "yes" instead of saying "no."

Do you feel like you spend most of your day saying "NO!" to your children? It seems like we are constantly saying no to this and no to that. Amazingly you can learn how to say "yes" most of the time to your children. But, you say, "I can't say yes to them, because what they want isn't good for them, or it's not what I want them to do." It seems we parents develop the "idiot no" habit early on.

The "idiot no:"

The "idiot no" is what I call it when we just automatically say "no" to everything. It's an easy answer. It's something we don't have to put much thought or effort into. And usually, we won't get into too much difficulty if we give the wrong response.

But the "idiot no" is also something that will cause a lot of frustration in your children. Let's say your child says, "Mom, Mom, Mom, I want a cookie." Immediately you think, *No, we're going to have dinner right now.* Instead of saying "no," think about it. Can they have a cookie? Yes. They actually can have a cookie. They just picked the wrong time. When can they have the cookie? Simply say, "You know what? You can have that cookie right after we have dinner. Do you know what we're going to have for dinner?"

If your child asks for gum and you don't want them to have it right now, you can say, "You know what? Right now I don't want you to have gum, because you have had three pieces already today. Instead of gum, what else would be good?" Your child might insist, "No, no, no, I want it now." You can say, "We won't have anything then." They might say, "I want something." You can say, "Okay, these are your options."

In some situations with your children, your answer must be "no." You have to say, "That's not possible today, but it is such a good idea, let's plan that for the day after tomorrow." You could still plan something else. Or they might say, "Mom, I want to eat this whole box of chocolates." Now, of course, you're not going to say "yes" to that. But you know what? You don't have to say "no" either. You could say, "You want to eat that whole box of chocolates? Well, so does your mom. But we don't eat a whole box of chocolates because for one thing, it would make us sick. For another thing, it's not good for your body. It has too much sugar and junk in it, but you could pick out one piece that you want. Let's cut it in half now. You can have this half now, and you can have the other half after you eat your lunch today." Or, "After dinner you can have the other half."

The older our kids get the more we have to take the time to think through our answers and not just use our *idiot no!* "Because I said so," just won't cut it anymore. There are so many life-choices they begin to make as they enter into their teen and young adult years. This isn't the time for parents to get lazy. We are expanding their responsibilities and their privileges almost on a daily basis. There are so many demands on us as parents to make decisions that can be vital to their growth and development as adults.

As your children begin to mature, this principle works the same. From keeping your new driver safe to them wanting to stay out late you are using the same principle as you did when they wanted gum before dinner. Instead of arguing with your teen about going to an inappropriate party, why not offer to have the party at your house? Many times we just say "no" and don't offer an explanation for our reasoning. We don't take the time to teach them the logic we used to reach our decision. It can make our children become angry and defiant. This is the time when many teens become rebellious, and parents often react by tightening their control and establishing more rules. The teen feels more restricted and may try to break free. It becomes a vicious cycle of demand and control. They are demanding their way and you are trying to control their actions. Parents must take the time to have conversations with their pre-teens and teenagers if they want to maintain a strong relationship during this stage of their growth.

This is the appropriate time during their growth and development for your pre-teen and teenager to make moves towards independence. It is normal and good for them to begin to draw away from your authority and make their own decisions. If they didn't want to be independent there would be something wrong.

The key to your teen making quality decisions partially rests on how you handle their demand for more and more independence. The more you use the "idiot no" in communicating with your teen the more difficult the transition from child to independent adult will become.

If you are parenting a teen right now, think of the times you have just said, "No" to them and if there might have been a better way to work through the situation you were facing. If we are willing to work and take the time to think about our response to our children, we can turn things around so we are saying "yes" instead of always saying "no."

Questions to Ponder

1. Give yourself a grade on a scale of one to ten (with one being lowest and ten being highest) of how often you say "yes" in comparison to how often you say "no."

2. Can you think of creative ways you can turn some of your *no's* into a positive *yes?* Write down a few ideas.

3. Give yourself a test: during the course of one day write down how many times you say "yes" and how many times you say "no."

Chapter 13
The Seed-Sowing Principle

If we try to protect our children from the
consequences they deserve, they are usually the ones
who turn around and have no respect or honor
for any boundaries and rules.

There are natural consequences in life. For instance, if you eat an apple that is not ripe or food that is not good, you will get a stomach ache. Not wearing a coat in cold weather could cause you to get sick. These are just a couple of natural consequences from doing the wrong things. Another truth is, *what your child sows is what your child will reap.* Galatians 6:7 teaches us: **Do not be deceived, God is not mocked; for whatever a man sows, that he will also reap.** You must train your child to know there are consequences that happen when he or she doesn't do the right thing.

Besides the natural consequences which can happen in the physical realm, there are other kinds of consequences our children can experience. These are the consequences which are imposed by their parents, teachers, and society for their bad behavior.

Consequences for inappropriate behavior.

Considering your child's bent and what he or she is capable of doing, there is a consequence for inappropriate behavior and/or performance at school. If your child brings home an "F," there is a consequence imposed by the parent. If your child does not complete their homework and turn it in on time, the teacher may impose a consequence. There are consequences imposed by society for breaking the law: a ticket or jail time. If your child is supposed to be home at a certain time and he doesn't come home by that time, there is a consequence.

There are certain guidelines we can use as parents in order to teach our children so that their choices come from within, instead of from without (correction from parents and/or society). Let's go through some of these guidelines.

1. Don't shield your child from consequences that ultimately would be a benefit to him or her.

As a part of raising children, I would say that most of us parents probably talk to our kids about the consequences for unacceptable behavior in our home. I would say (for the most part) we try to communicate guidelines for proper behavior and the consequences for missing the mark. Some parents have no problem dealing with unacceptable behavior and making sure their child reaps the appropriate consequences.

But, I would say that many times our challenge may come when others, outside our home, want to enforce their consequences on our children. That might be the time many parents have a desire to defend and protect. That might be the time we need to make sure we aren't protecting rather than allowing the consequence to teach our children.

If you went into a classroom and you saw your child sitting in the corner because he was being disciplined, don't say, "Oh no, poor Joey's not feeling good today, and that's why he is having a really hard day. It's my fault that he didn't get enough sleep, and I'm really sorry." Don't make excuses for his bad behavior and then try to get him out of the discipline. If we make excuses he will learn to place the responsibility of his bad behavior on others and not take responsibility for his own choices. Let him reap the consequences of his behavior. Bad behavior is a choice, no matter how we are feeling or what other circumstances are going on in our life.

I know that sometimes we would like to, but we cannot guard our children from every consequence in life. In fact, if we try to protect our children from the consequences they deserve, they are usually the ones who turn around and have no respect or honor for any boundaries and rules. They will take advantage of everyone and everything, thinking, *Momma or Daddy will always take care of me.*

2. Don't allow your child to blame others for his predicament.

Many people grow up believing they are a victim. When I was in the seventh grade, I had a girlfriend named Julie. Once when I spent the night at her house, we decided to sneak out and visit our boyfriends who lived only about a half mile away. So we left about midnight and all we did was throw rocks at their windows, got their attention, and said, "Hi! How are you doing?" They said, "Hi! How are you doing?" Then we said, "We'd better go now. Bye!" We went back to Julie's house, and that was it. It was all very innocent...except for the sneaking out and lying, of course!

On our way back to Julie's house, we saw her parents' car coming, so we hid in the trees. In the midst of walking home, it started to downpour. We were drenched by the time we got home, so we took off all of our clothes and threw them in the dryer. Then we ran into the basement and pretended we had been asleep. We thought we were going to fool them.

Her father came home and found us. "Julie, get up here," he said. We ran upstairs and lied to her father. We told him that we had gone for a walk. There was a runner's track just down the street. "We were bored so we ran around the track and got caught in the rain." Because Julie was with me and I was a pastor's daughter, her father believed us.

Years later, I had another girlfriend named Karen. I was saved and I wasn't doing anything wrong, but her mother instantly disliked me because I was a pastor's kid. She figured that all pastor's kids did negative things because where she grew up, all the pastors' kids were the wildest ones. The truth is I was the one who was keeping Karen straight. My role in her life was like a mother, telling her what not to do and what to do to live a holy life. But Karen's mother always blamed her bad behavior on me.

I share these two stories to show you how deceiving our thoughts can be towards our children's friends. One parent said, "Innocent," and we were guilty. The other parent said, "Guilty," and I was innocent of what I was being accused of doing. How often have we said about our children's friends, "They are the ones who always instigate the problems?" Sometimes we blame our children's friends for our child's behavior.

We cannot blame our children's friends for every bad thing that happens in their lives. Your children choose their friends. As a parent, I can gather around my children's friends whose parents believe in the same values and morals as we do. That doesn't tell me everything about their child, but it does give me some idea of what the parent would be putting into those children. Still this does not guarantee their child will make every choice correctly. Just because I raise my children by a certain standard doesn't mean they will always live up to that standard.

You cannot allow your child to become a victim in life, and you can't always blame other kids for what your child does. Your kid isn't always innocent while every other kid is guilty! My kids are normal. When they were little, they hit other kids, and so did yours (or they will). My kids were no more innocent and no more a "victim" than yours.

When Tasha was a year and a half, she would bite. It was amazing the response I got from different people. It was like biting was the sin of all sins, the evil of all evils. I said, "Excuse me, your child pulls Tasha's hair and Tasha bites." Which one was worse?

Don't be the "poor me" in life. Be the overcomer – the one who lives in continual victory! Don't raise your children to be the victim by defending them and blaming everyone else for their choices. The Bible is very clear: what you sow is what you will reap.

3. **Support your child in accepting a consequence.**

As parents, we need to encourage our children to keep a positive attitude in the midst of walking out the discipline that comes as a result of their actions. Support him by saying, "Sweetheart, you know the reason that you have to stay after school for three days in a row is because you chose not to do your homework." Don't get mad at them or sympathize with them. It's a good way to learn what the results are when you don't follow through. It's better for them to learn now than to lose a job later in life. Help your child understand the consequences of his attitudes and actions.

Don't ever let your child face a major consequence without support. I heard of a family whose daughter was going to marry someone they didn't want her to marry, so they refused to go to the wedding. The end of the story was the daughter went ahead with her plans regardless of her parents' wishes. You can either alienate yourself from your children or you can show acceptance and support. If they make a wrong choice and you keep the door open, then you can have open communication and a link back into their life. But if you slam the door, you will not have a place in their lives to be able to help when they need it. Many times you won't have any relationship at all.

As our kids get older there will be consequences they will face that we will not want to have to deal with, but we still need to love them. If a child ends up in jail, you can say, "It's a bummer that you broke the law. I don't like this, but it doesn't change the fact that I love you." Getting mad, hurt, or turning your back on them will not bring anything positive into your life or theirs.

I once knew of a mother who walked down the hall and found her son throwing scissors against the door. The mother got so angry that she could not respond to her child. She yelled, "Get in your room! Close the door and don't come out." She should have made an advance plan of the consequences for harming or breaking things, then she wouldn't have been caught off guard and not know how to respond.

It starts when they are little. If you are in a store and your child has a temper tantrum, screams and yells, you can prepare for that by thinking ahead of time, *what would I do in that situation?* Then, when the time comes you can stay calm, and *not react in an overly harsh manner.* Think ahead instead of always being caught off guard.

Think about ways to link their behavior to the consequence. It's a seed-sowing principle. If they sow something, they will reap something. If they go in the kitchen and sneak a candy bar and eat it, you can say, "Because you ate that candy bar without asking, that means you do not get any dessert for lunch or dinner." Link what they did to what they receive back.

141

Let's say that they scribbled all over the wall. The consequence of that is they have to wash it off. If they are disrespectful to an adult, my children would have been spanked. Or you could say, "Now, you have to stay in your room for five minutes and you don't get to be in the presence of the adult." Let the discipline be as close as possible to what the child did.

If your child uses one of his toys to hammer another object and it breaks, the consequence is to take away the toy that they were using destructively, or don't allow the child to play with any other toys for half an hour. If your kids are fighting over which video to watch, the consequence is to shut the television off.

We need to begin training our children at a young age to learn that they are going to be accountable for their actions. There are consequences; you have to let them reap what they have sown.

Questions to Ponder

1. Which of the three seed sowing principles are easiest for you to put into practice?

2. In what ways have you allowed your child to become a "victim" of circumstances? What can you do to make a change to help them accept responsibility for their actions?

3. Think of and write down a few age appropriate consequences you would use in training your children.

Chapter 14
Three Simple Rules

Not only do our children need to respect themselves and respect others, they need to learn a healthy respect for all the things God has given to us.

The Bible teaches us that God uses the simple things to confound the wise, and I have to say that the best parenting tools I ever used were extremely simple. You can read tons of parenting books filled with information, facts, data, and theories, but what will make the difference between a healthy, happy, well-adjusted child and one who is not are the three basic commands. They are:

1. You may not hurt *yourself.*
2. You may not hurt *others.*
3. You may not hurt *things.*

I used these three simple statements over and over as my children were growing up. I wanted to impress them upon their minds and plant them into their hearts. I wanted my children to remember them and remember to use them as a guideline in all their choices of life. The three basic commands are for all of us...for all of our lives. Everything fits within one of these three rules, which makes it better than trying to remember five million rules.

1. You may not hurt yourself.

From the first rule, children can learn how to judge, "Is this good for me to do? Will this hurt? Will this not hurt? Is this okay for my body? Is it not okay for my body?" These are a few examples of things that could hurt you. Don't take drugs. Don't drive if you are too tired. Don't smoke. Don't drive over the speed limits.

When Caleb was little and he climbed on something, I would say, "Caleb, you know something? I don't want you to jump off of that." He would ask, "Why?" I would answer, "Because you could hurt yourself." I was training him in a basic principle: *don't do things that would hurt yourself.*

If your child is around people who are mean, you

can say, "You know what? Those kinds of people hurt you." He may say, "What do you mean, they hurt me?" You can answer, "They keep you from growing up strong. They hurt your spiritual life with God because they don't honor God." You are giving them something to think about as they make choices in life.

You can say, "Don't hang around with angry people, lest you learn their ways. That attitude, that negative way of thinking and acting, will hurt you in your growth as a mighty man or woman of God."

Your child is learning how to make choices. If there is an excessive number of rules to try to remember, children can make excuses and not take responsibility. As you continue to reinforce the rule *you may not hurt yourself* you are training them, "Don't hurt yourself mentally, physically, socially, or financially." This basic principle will become a part of who they are.

2. You may not hurt others.

This basic command is especially good when you have little ones in your home. When Caleb and Tasha were small and at the age when they would hit each other, I would say to them, "No, you don't hurt other people." Rather than just say, "No, we don't hit others," I would say, "We don't hurt other people." We have to let them know that not only are they doing something that is wrong, but it is also hurtful to someone else.

Another way we can hurt people is by saying mean words. When we say mean, hurtful words over and over and over again, it hurts people. It's amazing how simple discipline will become because you can say, "What did that do? Did it hurt him? Did it hurt someone when you said those words?" Once we say certain words, they cannot be recalled. We have to teach our children to be very careful about the words they use and the hurtful affect they can have on others.

When your children are angry and they act out their anger, you can tell them, "That hurts people when you act like that. It's just not the right way to act towards people because it makes them feel hurt." To hit others, deliberately exclude them, call them a name, or hang up the phone on a person *hurts* them.

Teenagers can be especially nasty to each other. I remember when I was in eighth grade, several girls had a slumber party and I was a brand-new kid. They all called me from the party and said, "Hi," and laughed and made me feel left out. Later, many of the girls from the party called or came to me and apologized. They had been taught growing up, *don't hurt people*, but because of the peer pressure, no one stood up and said, "No, this is not the right way to act."

If we train our children to understand that we don't hurt people, they won't become people who do hurtful things. We can help our children be the kind, loving people God has created them to be.

3. You may not hurt things.

Not only do our children need to respect themselves and respect others, they need to learn a healthy respect for all the *things* God has given to us. In order to be productive stewards of God's blessings, we need to take care of what He has given to us. We need to teach and train our children to take care of *things*. You may want to use another word such as destroy or ruin, but the idea is that we are not destructive in our actions towards the things God has given us.

If a child has a baseball bat and they are swinging it in the living room you say, "No, don't do that." If the child says, "Well, it's not hurting me and it's not hurting another person," you can say, "Yes, but you can hurt things. Look at what could happen. You could hit the ball through the window. *We don't hurt things.*" If your child is jumping from the couch, to the chair, to the floor, you say, "Please don't do that because you can hurt things." When you are driving in the car and they are doing things that could damage something, again you can say, "No, we don't hurt things. We don't beat up on things. We don't pound on things."

As you continue to sow the words *we don't hurt things* into your child, when they grow up they will begin to think of the consequences of their actions. One day when your child is outside playing baseball right next to your huge picture window, just as he is about ready to swing the bat, he will suddenly realize, "Wait a minute. I could *hurt something.* I could break the window." You see the goal is to have them change, not because you told them, "Don't play baseball in the front yard," but because they think, *I could hurt something.* As you build their pattern of thinking by teaching and training your children, they will become more aware of hurting things. Our goal is to raise children who are responsible, kind, and thoughtful people. The three basic commands go far in achieving our goal to have our children become mature, responsible adults who do not hurt themselves, hurt others, or hurt things.

Questions to Ponder

1. Write out the three basic commands.

2. Which of the three areas would be the most important for you to focus on with your child at this stage of his life?

3. How can you creatively begin to teach your child in this area?

Chapter 15
Mother May I?

As we raise our children to be obedient we are giving them one of the most important character traits we can instill.

Have you ever had a job that demanded so much of you that you couldn't possibly do all the tasks required? After all, there are only twenty-four hours in a day! Or, besides being a parent, do you also work full-time, take care of all the household chores, volunteer at your church, and make sure you are fresh and ready for a special date with your mate? Sometimes the goals we set for ourselves or those set for us by others are just *not* possible. We are just not capable of doing the job!

Sadly, some of *us* demand our children do things that they just are not capable of doing either. I mean, we tell them to do twelve things at once: "Okay, first take out the garbage. Then clean out the garbage can. Come back in the house and vacuum the carpet. Dust, clean up your room, and put all of your toys away. Make your bed just right, then come downstairs and start the dinner."

We give them a long list of tasks at once, or we are not reasonable in what we request them to do because we don't consider their age or their ability. We need to set *obeyable* limits.

Don't stretch them to the max.

There is only so much a child is able to obey, so why stretch them to the limit? Be smart and ask yourself, *how can I work with my children so that I am constantly training them to obey, rather than provoking them to disobedience?* Ephesians 6:4 says: **Fathers, do not provoke your children to wrath, but bring them up in the training and admonition of the Lord.** This verse also includes mothers. We can demand so much from our children that they get frustrated and discouraged instead of being encouraged and trained to accomplish what they are capable of doing.

Well, Most of the Time!

Now of course, there are also those times when you are not giving him enough! You think that your child is able to handle a certain amount of responsibility. But you know something? He actually has the ability to go further. He just needs to stretch himself a little bit more. That is when you are able to increase what you are asking him to accomplish. You will be able to go a little bit further, but only if you have taught him how to obey and you are sensitive to lead him by the string principle instead of pushing him all the time.

Guidelines for setting *obey-able* limits:
1. Be clear in your request.

In setting limits that our children can obey, we must be very clear in what we ask our child to do. There are things that you ask your child to do when you should be telling them. Instead of saying, "Would you do this?" we need to say, "This is what you are going to do."

I think we have gotten the idea that we have to talk *commando* to our kids to make them obey us. Some parents think if we talk nice we lose our authority and then our kids won't obey us. As parents, we should not have the attitude, "Kid, obey me." Instead, our attitude should be, "In this house we are a team." In our household, as parents we are the boss, but our whole family is a team in taking care of the needs of our home. Out of the abundance of the heart of my children, I want their love for me to communicate, "Okay, let's do it!" I want to have my requests easily obeyed. When a need comes up state your instruction with a big smile on your face, and it will sound a lot more like a request than a demand.

2. Be clear about the timeframe in which you expect your child to complete the task.

Many times we are in a hurry and don't clearly communicate with our children what our expectations are. We need to be very clear in what we want them to do and when we want them to do it. Don't say something like, "Go clean your room right now. Hurry up. Move it. I want it done now." How does that help a child know what you want so he can obey what he is supposed to do?

Why not say something like, "Sweetheart, I looked at your room and it needs some attention. I know you just got home from school, but before dinnertime, get your room clean, neat, and looking sharp. Do you need more specifics?" You were very clear. Their expected time of completion is before dinnertime. You could even go a little further, "Remember, dinner is at 6:00."

It always helps to ask a question to invite their input. I am giving them the option to tell me if there is anything that would hinder them from obeying. I don't want to give them the option to say, "No, I don't agree, so I don't think I will do that." What I am saying is, don't always give directives that cannot be discussed and modified if there is a more immediate need of which you are not aware. Not only does that come across as demanding, but you set both yourself (and your child) up for a problem.

If your husband said to you, "I want dinner right now," how would you feel? Instead of saying, "Sweetheart, will you take out the garbage?" say something like, "Hey, Honey, before you leave for work today, could you grab the garbage and throw it in the garbage can?" This way you have given him clear time limits, but you have also made your request with a big smile on your face. It works when you work as a team instead of seeing yourself as the sergeant at arms!

3. Make the request once and reward quick obedience.

When you make a clear request and you give an absolute time frame for when it needs to be done, you shouldn't repeat yourself over and over. This happens to most of us. "Do this. Do that." If we repeat ourselves, we're guilty of whining rather than making a clear request with the details they need to accomplish the task.

Once you have made a request and clearly outlined what needs to be done and given a time frame, acknowledge quick obedience with a reward. It can be anything from a loving touch, or a smile, to saying "good job," or receiving a special privilege. As we train our children from a young age to obey quickly they will become teens and young adults who will have success in school and the workforce later in life.

4. Follow through to quick obedience.

The worst thing we can do for our kids is not demand they follow through when asked to do a task. Even though we don't want to have to keep repeating ourselves and following our children around until the job is done, we do need to be aware of their progress. Many parents keep talking, asking, yelling, and demanding things of their kids, but they don't take the time to follow through. When your children obey, follow through with a reward. When they don't obey, follow through with the appropriate discipline. We want our children to know that it isn't an option to disobey.

5. Be willing to stop whatever you are doing to follow up on obedience.

This is a huge issue with many parents! You must be

willing to stop what you're doing at any time to bring about obedience in your children. This means that sometimes you have to give up being comfortable, or give up some of your fun and relaxation. Parenting is a full-time, 24/7 kind of job!

Let's say you are tired and you just sat down and got comfortable with your popcorn and TV program, and you ask your child to do something. You have made it very clear what you want and you gave a time limit. You said it as a request, with a smile on your face. You did everything right, but if you don't follow through, you just dropped the ball! It doesn't take more than once for your child to think, *if I just wait long enough Mom will forget.* So you have to *remember* what you said and then *follow through* on what you said.

As a parent, you really have to be aware and follow up on your child when you are busy. If your child hasn't obeyed, you don't have to get upset with him at that time, but you do have to get up and say, "Now, Johnny, come with me. Remember what Mommy asked you to do?" You have to make him follow through and obey. It is our responsibility to lead our children to obedience. That's just what we have to do, and that means we cannot be lazy moms. We have to be willing to move, to stop everything to follow up, and train our children to be obedient.

6. Don't give your child more tasks than they can handle at one time.

Depending on the age of our children, we need to ask them to do only as many tasks as they can remember to accomplish at one time. They may only be old enough to do one thing at a time. You know what your child can do and what he is not capable of doing. Don't put so much on him that he gets frustrated or forgets something. Don't set her up for failure. Unless it's something that has been a repetitive thing, you need to limit the number of things she is doing at one time.

Sometimes we think our child should remember everything she is supposed to do. But don't get mad at her if she forgets to do one of the things she was supposed to do, and think she just disobeyed you. She might have been in the middle of completing item number one and then started reading an old magazine or got distracted and started cleaning a drawer instead. We can't put every lapse in the category of disobedience. Sometimes they are just being forgetful, distracted, or human...just like us!

You and I do the same thing when we are cleaning or picking things up. We get distracted. Don't discipline your child for the very thing that we all have been guilty of doing. Just train them how to keep their thoughts focused in order to complete tasks one, two, and three. Leave him a list or have a check-off sheet on the refrigerator, or, as I mentioned earlier, just give him one task at a time if that is appropriate for his age.

7. Make obeying fun!

Be creative and fun in helping your children complete their responsibilities. If you have two children, you might tell one, "You get to vacuum both rooms. Okay? Then you get to tag your sister and she gets to dust as fast as she can. Then she gets to come and tag you while you run back in there and pick up all the books. Let's see how fast you can do it." They can both have several things that they get to do. You can have a list and if it's a tag game, say to them, "Let's see how fast we can get it done."

This does not work for everybody, but with your family it might work to make a game out of it. If your children play really well together, you can turn cleaning into a game. You can make obedience a game where they work together. In teaching your children to help each other complete their tasks you are also teaching a wonderful skill that will help them all of their lives. They will develop the skill of working together as a team.

As we raise our children to be obedient we are giving them one of the most important character traits we can instill. Not only will this help them in their walk with Christ, but in all their future relationships of life. Quick obedience can even save their lives in certain situations. God places a very high value on obedience. In raising happy, healthy children who love God, obedience is vital, and when we set *obey-able* limits we make it possible to obey and bring success instead of failure.

Questions to Ponder

1. Can you think of any ways you are demanding too much of your child in a particular area of their life?

2. Of the seven guidelines for setting *obey-able* limits, which area would be your strength?

3. Which of the seven guidelines would be your weakness? How can you improve in this area?

Chapter 16
C.O.R.R.E.C.T.I.O.N.

Our children are all going to miss the mark in some way at different stages of their growth.

Correct, discipline, rebuke, chastise...there are many ways to say it, and just as many ways to administer correction to our children. The distinguishing difference will be in the way we approach discipline. Are you simply tired of their funky attitude or bad behavior and want to lash out? Do you react out of frustration or do you have a well-thought-out plan of action when it comes to disciplining your children?

Again, I would like to use an acronym to describe "correction" as it relates to helping our children grow up to be the champions God has ordained them to be:

C	Clarity
O	Obedience
R	Right attitude
R	Restoration
E	Explanation
C	Consistency
T	Thoughtfulness
I	Immediate discipline
O	Out of sight
N	Neutral objects

"C" – Clarity

Clearly define the limitations and the boundaries of what you expect from your child. The three basic commands, which were mentioned earlier, are helpful in setting the boundaries for discipline:

1. Don't hurt *yourself*.
2. Don't hurt *others*.
3. Don't hurt *things*.

As my children were growing up, I was consistent in

the use of certain words. When they were misbehaving and I wanted to teach them they couldn't hit their sibling, I would say, "No, you may not hit your sister. We don't hurt people." We need to use the same words consistently in speaking to a young child to help them learn what is acceptable and what is not.

"O" – Obedience

Sometimes we are unwise in how we direct our children because we'll say, "Pick up the things in your room," and they clean up half of their room. They don't finish. We must make sure they will follow through all the way to complete what you ask them to do.

I will say it again: as moms we cannot give directions from our easy chair! We have to be *moving* moms to make sure that our children completely obey us. You might be a mom who says, "Obey me. Get going. Do this." I have felt like doing that many times myself. But there are other ways we can work with our children through humor, by being creative, having fun, and playing.

I talked about obeying quite a lot in the last chapter, so I won't belabor the point. I just want to say again that in discipline we have to be willing to follow through with the appropriate discipline when our children are disobedient.

"R" – Right attitude

Philippians 2:14 says: **Do all things without complaining and disputing.** That means we train our kids to say, "Yes, Mom, I'll do it," at the same time making sure they have a right attitude while they do what they were asked. If your child is always grumbling and murmuring, he is not being obedient with a right attitude and that needs to be corrected. We cannot allow our children to do the right actions with a wrong heart. A good attitude has to accompany the right action.

For instance, say you ask your child to pick up his toys and get ready for dinner. He begins to do what you asked, but all the while he is grumbling about his friend who doesn't have to clean up his toys, or about his sister never having to pick up her toys. Technically, he is obeying you, but his heart is not willing. With willing obedience, a child will complete what you ask him to do without complaining or grumbling.

"R" – Restoration

II Corinthians 2:7-8 says: *So that, on the contrary, you ought rather to forgive and comfort him, lest perhaps such a one be swallowed up with too much sorrow. Therefore I urge you to reaffirm your love to him.*

These verses are talking about a brother who was removed from the church because of sin. Paul is saying; *Restore him so that the devil doesn't swallow him up.* As parents, we need to restore our children. After we have corrected them, disciplined them, and trained them, we need to restore them so they don't get bitter or discouraged in their heart.

Our children are all going to miss the mark in some way at different stages of their growth. After the discipline is over and regardless of your child's age, you have to physically communicate acceptance and forgiveness with them as best you can. You need to take the time to say, "I love you. I'm so glad that you are mine. I'm happy that you are a part of our family." This will restore them and build them up. You will help them be able to move on and not allow past failures to continue to keep them captive.

We have to be the builders of our children's confidence. We are the ones who can bring restoration and wholeness. Be sure to follow up every act of discipline with a few moments of affirmation of your love and support.

"E" – Explanation

Never leave a child confused as to why they are being disciplined. You have to talk with them and explain your perspective on the reason they are being disciplined. You might say, "The reason that you are being disciplined is because the tone of your voice when you spoke with me was very disrespectful."

Depending on the age of your child you might need to teach them the definition of the word *disrespectful*. Break it down as clearly as possible so they will understand. You can build a bridge with good communication or you can build a wall of misunderstanding and mistrust by unclear or non-communication.

Sometimes you will need to correct the tone in which your children speak to you or to others. For example, when my children were small, I would say, "When you said, '*I don't like that*,' we don't talk like that in our house. If you don't like something, you can nicely say, '*May I have something else, please*?'" I wanted to make sure they understood and got a clear picture of why they were being corrected.

It's easy for all of us to say, "Don't do this. Don't do that." But, if your children don't know what they are supposed to be doing or why they should not do something, they can't make good decisions. Now, we have to keep a good balance. I'm not saying you have to explain every little detail of your life, but if there is a point of confusion, clearly explain it.

Years ago we cared for the daughters of friends as they traveled out of the country. During one such occasion, I asked one of the girls to do something and she said, "No." I sent her upstairs to her room and I said, "I'll be up in a minute to talk to you." I went upstairs and as I talked to her about what had happened I was amazed at her perception. She had a completely different picture of the situation and did not even see how she had disobeyed. I could not believe the difference of what she had seen compared with what I had seen.

Now I could have gone upstairs and just spanked her for being disobedient. I had agreement and permission from her parents, and had spanked her previously when she was with us. So I could have gone ahead and spanked her without talking first. But I wanted to talk with her and find out what was going on and why she was acting that way. It was a good thing because I realized that we completely missed each other in the communication. She wasn't being disobedient after all; she simply didn't hear what I was asking her to do.

Not only does there have to be an explanation as to why a person should be disciplined, but many times as we talk we find out it was a total misunderstanding and really not disobedience. How many times have you had an issue with a friend or your spouse only to find out you totally misunderstood what they said or did? It happens with our kids also. We have to take the time to talk and find out what everyone is really saying.

"C" – Consistency

Consistency is so important when it comes to effective discipline. But you have to make it a point to remember to be consistent. You have to think about what your plan of action is for certain situations and ages of your children.

Remember the Ten to One rule and then put it into practice every day. Make the effort to remember *the three basic commands* and make those a part of how you speak with and teach your children. You have to take the time to *fill their tank*, tell them how awesome they are, and how much you love them.

You also have to spank them when you have told them you were going to. You have to be consistent day in and day out, doing the same things over and over. You have to say the same words over and over. You have to let your children know their boundaries and what is acceptable in your household. And the only way they will know and understand your expectations for them, is when you are consistent.

Galatians 6:9 says: ***And let us not grow weary while doing good, for in due season we shall reap if we do not lose heart.*** Don't faint, don't give up, don't get weary of doing the right things, but persevere and you will see the fruit of your labor in your children's lives.

"T" – Thoughtfulness

As parents, we must recognize that we can wound our child's spirit. We can discourage him and bring about a broken spirit. When I think of the word *thoughtful*, I think of Proverbs 18:14: *The spirit of a man will sustain him in sickness, but who can bear a broken spirit;* and Proverbs 17:22: *A merry heart does good, like medicine, but a broken spirit dries the bones.*

There are times in the midst of correction that you need to stop and say, "Wait a minute. Come here. Let Mom hug you," or, "Instead of going through all this, let's go get some ice cream." Sometimes we get so serious-minded we become very heavy in our communication with our kids. Sometimes their actions are simply a plea for some attention. They get the negative attention their behavior demands because they don't always know how to ask for the positive attention they need.

Think about how your child would respond if next time you need to discipline him for misbehaving you said, "You know what? That wasn't a great way for you to act and Mom doesn't like it when you do that, but right now I think we just need to go outside and run and play." You can be sure their tank just got filled; you built them up, and their behavior is going to follow. Do you see how you can still be consistent in correcting them, yet not wound their heart?

Proverbs 12:18 says: *There is one who speaks like the piercings of a sword, but the tongue of the wise promotes health.* Say thoughtful words to your child – good words, loving words, powerful things – and watch the difference in their attitude and willingness to do what is right.

"I" – Immediate discipline

Discipline is not something you can put off or take care of at a more convenient time. The longer you wait, the harder it will be to take care of it. If you wait too long, you may think, "Why deal with it now? They probably forgot anyway."

One important reason it's important to discipline immediately is because your kids *will* forget. If you discipline for something they did two days ago, they'll think, "What did I do?" They won't get the benefit of really understanding what you are trying to teach. Plus, if you don't discipline immediately, there's a chance you will forget why you wanted to discipline them in the first place.

You have to immediately address the situation with them or you will lose the moment of really teaching and training them what you want them to learn. Now there are a few situations that you might deal with later because it might be inappropriate, but if at all possible, deal with it immediately.

Also, don't put off discipline for later with a threat like, "Wait until your father comes home. You're really going to get it then!" Moms need to rise up and take care of issues and not make Dad come home to be the bad guy. There may be times when a group discussion is needed and it is okay to say, "We need to talk about this with Dad when he gets home." But, don't delay discipline like spankings or time outs until a later time because you don't want to deal with it.

"O" – Out of sight

Out of sight means to deal with your children privately – never in front of anyone else. I don't mean your baby can't be corrected in front of Grandma. With smaller children, up to a year or a year-and-a-half, the discipline would be a word or a gentle slap on their hand if they got into something they should not have gotten into. I would never discipline a three-year-old in front of anyone else, including their brothers and sisters. It should be a private situation.

When our children were small, Caleb would cry after I had disciplined him, and Tasha would silently enter the room, as if to say, "What can I do?" (We didn't allow her to be there while we disciplined). She communicated concern and love to build him up. So I would let her come in and hug him after he had been disciplined. She was young and he was able to deal with it, but we always corrected our children individually.

If you are in public and your child needs to be disciplined, quickly find a private area. That might have to be all the way out to your car. It might be that you need to go in a dressing room or a bathroom so you can deal with your child privately. Don't yell at your kids on the way out of the store, saying things like, "Shut up." I've seen too many parents yell at their kids, yank on their arms, and push them around in public. Their little spirits get so wounded when we are insensitive.

In adult terms, if you or I were walking down the mall with our husband and he said, "Shut up," what would we do? We would feel humiliated or angry or bad about being talked to that way. Hopefully we don't ever talk that way with each other, but wisdom calls for a private place of rebuke and correction. We have to discipline in a way that does not humiliate, put down, or break our children's spirit.

"N" – Neutral object

A neutral object is needed when you use the *rod of*

correction. The Bible very clearly teaches us to use the *rod of correction.* ***Foolishness is bound up in the heart of a child; the rod of correction will drive it far from him*** (Proverbs 22:15). Our hand is not a neutral object. Our hand is to be used to love, hug, touch kindly, and comfort our children. A neutral object is something we can use to bring correction that is separate from us. It is not a part of our body, and when our children see us they don't connect us with the *rod of correction.* They connect us with loving touch.

In our household we had "the paddle." You need a paddle of some sort, depending on the age of your child. You can get different sizes, shapes, and thicknesses of paddles. I wouldn't use the same *rod of correction* on my three-year-old as I would on a twelve-year-old. Many have used a wooden spoon as their *rod of correction,* but I have found the wooden spoon will bruise. A ping-pong paddle won't bruise.

Wisdom tip: Never use your *rod of correction* when you are angry or when you have reached your limit. Don't ever use it to discipline at a time when you are not in control of your emotions, because then you can quickly move into abusing rather than disciplining your child. Don't let yourself get to that place. The reason that you get to that place is because you allow three, four, or more incidents go by when the child should have been disciplined previously. That's usually the time that your anger or frustration is heightened. If you're in that place, you should just say, "I need some time to cool off, excuse me." Take the rod and give yourself a few minutes to cool down and get your perspective back.

I hope you noticed that I put spanking at the end of

the list of discipline measures. I know there is a lot of controversy about spanking in our liberal society today. I just go with what the Bible teaches. Remember the Word says: *Foolishness is bound up in the heart of a child; the rod of correction will drive it far from him* (Proverbs 22:15). I want to obey God and trust His ways above my own. At the same time, spanking was often the last method of discipline I chose to use with my children. I would use spanking for very serious issues, such as outright rebellion. There are certain *foolish* attitudes I want to drive far from my children.

Questions to Ponder

1. Think about your style of discipline. Is there one key from the ten listed that stood out to you?

2. Are you clear with your child about your expectations and the consequences for disobedience?

3. Do you consciously take the time for restoration with your child after you discipline them? If not, take a moment next time to make sure they know you love them unconditionally.

Chapter 17
Are You a Guilty Mom?

There has never been a command in the Bible that says moms need to be at home full-time or that they need to be working outside the home.

Years ago, when our children were young, Casey and I began discussing what we believed the role of a mom was in today's society. Many career women had just begun to start their families and had the hard choice of daycare versus being a stay-at-home mom. Home schooling had just begun to make its mark as a major choice for women.

In the church, lines began to become very clearly drawn: It was said by some that if you had children and continued in the workforce, your children would grow up to become dysfunctional. The new catchphrase "latch-key kids" was all the rage, and moms were caught in the middle of the debate.

One day Casey made the statement to me, "You talk to women – from the full-time working mom to the full-time home mom – and many women are feeling so guilty." I was always being asked, "Should I work outside the home?" Or, "Should I be a stay-at-home mom?" There was so much confusion and with that came a great deal of guilt.

I didn't want to base my response to these women out of my preference or just give them my opinion. I took the time to seek out answers and found that there are strong arguments for both sides. I would like to present that information to you so that you can make your own decision based on a variety of thoughts.

The stay-at-home mom:

I found there were several reasons women think they should stay home. Here are the most commonly held reasons:

- Studies say children are happier when moms are home.
- Studies say the kids of stay-at-home moms are

going to be more successful.
- Many women believe they are the only one who can give their child what he or she really needs.
- Some women say, "I cannot make enough money to pay for daycare, so I need to stay home."
- "My mom stayed at home."
- "I'm not trained to do anything but stay at home."

Some of us believe we have to stay home because if we are not there, our children will become wild and crazy. They will get involved in drugs, they'll bring ungodly people to your home, and then some evil thing will happen to them.

Yes, it may be true that if you are not there to supervise your children, they may have too much extra time and they could make a choice to do something wrong. It's true they might make friends with the wrong kind of people if you aren't there to guide their choices. There are seeds of truth and seeds of lies in all of these thoughts. But, my question is this, is it possible those choices could happen whether you work outside the home or not?

The working mom:

Some of the reasons women give for working outside of the home are:
- "I want to work; I like working."
- "We need the money."
- "I'm a single mom."
- "My career would pass me up if I took a break."
- "My mom worked."
- "I'd go crazy if I were home every day."
- "My husband wants me to work."

The bottom line is there are many reasons women give to continue working after having children. The husband wants the money. His mom worked so he wants you to work. "We want to send our children to the right schools, we want them to have all the right clothes, and we want the right house."

I know many women who work full-time positions because they want a certain house, certain furniture, certain carpet, certain everything in their house, so they are willing to say, "I know I am sacrificing time with my kids, but I really need to work to have the lifestyle I want."

There are single moms who stay home and single moms who work. Single moms who stay home usually have a struggle. Most single moms feel guilty because they have to work, but they don't have other options.

Which is best?

There have been times in history when most women worked and the children were raised by grandmothers and other family members. Many worked in the fields, or washed clothing, or cooked meals from sun up to sun down. It may not have been "a job in town" but it was a full-time job nonetheless.

Then there have been times when mothers didn't work outside the home at all. They stayed home all day and lived the "June Cleaver" lifestyle of making breakfast, lunch, and dinner and had fresh cookies at the door when the children got home from school, all the while sporting their frilly white apron and pearls.

I can't tell you which is right and which is wrong because bad things have happened throughout history when women were working outside the home and when they weren't working outside the home. There has never been a command in the Bible that says moms need to be at home full-time or that they need to be working outside the home. This is not a Biblical issue with a "yes" or "no" answer. Results of studies of stay-at-home moms versus working moms show various results – both pros and cons each way. So who is right?

Ask yourself these questions: Were your parents right in what they did? Are you now following their example? Did your mother stay at home out of guilt or work outside the home because of outside pressures?

If your mom didn't make her choices for the right reasons, and you are following in her footsteps, you could be following a wrong path. Maybe your mother followed the tradition that was in her family, or perhaps you are doing something without knowing why, but you think, *I have to because my mom did it, and that means it is okay.* It can be very confusing to follow someone or a tradition without thinking or praying about it for yourself.

There is a right way for some people and a right way for others. What is best for one person may not be the same for another. Personally, I believe a certain way, so I have to be very careful to not try to make you think only the way I think.

We each have to make our own decision based on the facts of our life and the individual choices we need to consider. We all have different circumstances and different needs, so the only way to determine what is best for our family is through careful consideration, asking God and asking great, godly friends for input, and then making our own decision.

I have thought, *okay, God, I believe there are valid reasons that some women work outside the home and there is also validity to many of the things that I have heard about the reasons mothers need to stay at home.* There are reasons to give your child the stability of being a stay-at-home mom and the amount of time you can give into your child's life. But there is also something about the working mom who says, "You know something? If I stayed home all the time, I'd go crazy." If she did go crazy, what would she be giving her child? Craziness!

You might think, *well, then she shouldn't have had kids.* That would mean that over fifty percent of the people who have children shouldn't have them, because many women *and* men can't handle being with their children twenty-four hours a day. Children are great, but they are so daily. The demands on you to perform, to love them, to be patient, to be kind, to discipline them properly, to teach and train them are constant and always present. The demands can be exceptionally big.

Some parents believe, "I do a better job with those demands when I get out of the house for a while." They aren't the best for their children on a full-time basis. They need to get outside the home for a few hours a day and focus on something else.

Questions for determining the route for you:

So what should you do? Here are a few questions to help you decide the best route for you to take:

1. What do you really want to do?

No one can tell you that. Your husband can't tell you. Your friends can't tell you. I can't tell you. Is it in your heart to be home full-time with your children, or is it in your heart to have some kind of outside job? What's in your heart? You really have to take some time to pray and seek God's plan for this season of your life.

You have to consider what the best is for your family during this particular season of your life. Think about the long-term benefits or problems that will result. Whatever your decision, you will have to live it out every day, and you have to get your heart in line with the decision so you aren't dealing with resentment and guilt later on.

2. What do you feel is the will of God for your life?

God's will for you is more important than your own desires. Do you feel you have a calling on your life to do a certain job? Are you trained in a particular field and feel it is God's plan for you to continue working in it? Don't go to God and say, "What is *Your* will?" without being honest with yourself first. You must first know your own desire. Then go to God and say, "God, this is what I'm considering. This is what is going on with my family." (Of course, He already knows.) But, talk to Him about what is in your heart to do and ask Him to give you the peace and wisdom to make great decisions based on His will for you.

Take the time to lay it at His feet. Ask for His wisdom. You can say, "God, You know the needs of my family. You know more than just the outer needs. You know the spiritual, the mental, the physical, the social, and the intellectual needs of my family. You know if my child will do well if I put him in a daycare, and you also know if he will not do well in a daycare." Then expect an answer. God cares about the details of our lives and wants to show us the best way for us. Get the will of God. He is not hard to hear. After you pray, let the peace of God direct you.

3. What does your mate think and feel?

Agreement is the foundation of a happy family. Agreement between a husband and wife is a key to the success of any household. It matters a lot what your husband thinks and feels about your role as a home-mom versus being a mom who works outside the home, because you need to be in agreement.

What if you want to stay at home and your husband says, "No way. I believe you should be working full-time." You could say, "You know, Sweetheart, I thought that way, too, but let me show you something. These are some things that I've thought, considered, and prayed about," and you tell him your very clear picture of why you want to be home full-time.

On the other hand, you may feel you need to work outside the home and your husband may say, "You need to be home." You could say, "You know, Sweetheart, these are the things I've been thinking about. Let me show you." Then you can give him a clear picture of your thoughts so you have something to discuss.

When you take the time to prayerfully consider what you desire and what you believe God's plan is for your role in the family, your husband will realize that you are not just coming up with a spur-of-the-moment thought by saying, "I want to do this." He will realize that you have thought it out, planned, and meditated on what you believe is the best thing for your family.

Now, there is the possibility that your husband is not going to support your decision no matter what you do. In an extreme example, if you have a husband who does absolutely nothing at home and you have five children under five, you might have a problem, especially if you want to work outside the home, but he doesn't want you to. You will go crazy trying to get everything done, because he probably will not be supportive of your decision. If you work forty-hours-a-week, plus an hour traveling each way, that would be a ten-hour day outside the home. That might not work for you.

But if you have one child who is two years old and your husband loves to do anything and everything, that's an entirely different situation. If he is supportive and helpful, both of you as a team can make things work for your household. The key to your success is the agreement between husband and wife.

4. Ask yourself, "How much of <u>me</u> is needed in my job?

It really matters what kind of job you want to pursue. If you are in real estate, you will have calls every hour of the day and on weekends, too. There are many jobs where you take your work home with you. There are highly stressful situations that take long hours at the job and consume your thoughts after working hours also. Is it possible for you to have a job where you go in, do your thing, and walk away?

I have found that even for myself, in ministry, I can only put so much into my work and still be able to have a clear mind at home. To me it's not just a job, it is a calling. But I can only do so much, and I've had to recognize that and cut out some things. When my children were young, I had to let go of some of my responsibilities and let someone else who had more time handle the different areas of the ministry.

We have to recognize the season of life we are in and

how that will affect our choices. If I have three small children at home, maybe I can work one or two afternoons a week. If I am in the season that all my children are at school, I have more possibilities.

5. Ask yourself, "Would I rather volunteer?"

Do you want to get out of your home one or two days a week just because you need the break? What about volunteering? Would you honestly rather volunteer? Sometimes you may think, *I just need a break from the house and the kids. I really need to use my gifting and would like some way to keep it fresh.* But maybe you just need to do something new and you could do it in other ways, rather than taking on the responsibilities of a job.

There are endless ways to volunteer and use your creativity or skills. You can help out at your church office, help with different events, work at the local food bank or shelter, or even start a Bible study or prayer group once a month. There are wonderful ways to keep yourself in touch with other adults and stay current in your skills if you would rather volunteer than get a job.

6. Ask yourself, "What can I truly handle?"

Can you handle working a forty-hour-a-week job? Can you handle forty hours outside of your home and then go home and handle your children, your household chores, and be a good wife?

Most studies show that personal hobbies are low on a full-time working mom's priority list. Personal time for going out to lunch, being with people, having people over to your home for dinner and things like that drop because you don't have the time. So the question is, *can you handle that kind of a lifestyle?* I like parties and I love having people over to our home, but other women don't enjoy that. What do you want to do? What can you realistically handle in a day, in a week, in a month? Can you give to your family, maintain your relationship with God, keep up with your job, and have anything left for yourself?

Why we do the things we do...

When Casey and I asked some women, "Why do you stay home?" they said, "Well, you know what could happen to my children if I wasn't there." I want to say, "Wait a minute, are you staying home out of fear? Are you motivated out of fear that if you are not at home to take care of your children, something will happen to them? Who says something won't happen when you are there?"

Some people have said, "I give my children all this quality time." Studies show that women who are home full-time don't necessarily give their children more time than those who work full-time. They think that since they are present, they don't have to give quality time. Are you giving quantity but not quality? How much do you play with your kids? How much do you read with your children? How much time do you spend doing activities with them?

Some mothers will say, "I am a full-time home mom," yet they are doing their own thing. They get up and do what they want to do. They have their whole schedule outlined and they fit their kids into it. It's really not any different than if they were in daycare. They have them scheduled into so many classes and programs they might as well be in daycare all day.

When a working mom comes home, she recognizes, "My kids did not get me all day," and usually she will consider, "I need to sit down and be with my children." The opposite is true of some women who are home full-time. "I'm around all the time," yet their children don't get their attention all the time!

Are you really being the kind of mom that you want to be? Are you in the place and location where you want to be, or are you doing what you are doing out of guilt?

Some women don't want to work because they are afraid of the workforce, yet they hate being home. Their fear of going out into the workforce is stronger than their distaste for being at home. Simply because you have chosen to stay at home, it doesn't mean you are doing anything in your home. Some women don't make the most of the time they have at home. Being at home full-time is a job, and you need to consider it as such.

Each year Casey and I put our goals and plans together for the year. Then at the end of the year we discuss if we successfully fulfilled the goals we had planned to reach. As a full-time home mom, what are your goals, plans, and purposes for your home? Have you written it down? Have you planned, and are you fulfilling your goals? If not, are you just letting life pass you by? Be honest and give yourself a strong reality check. Ask yourself, "Why am I choosing what I am choosing? Why am I choosing to stay home full-time?" Or, "Why am I choosing to work outside my home?"

Here are some questions to help you really think through the possibilities:

- What are the ages of my children?
- What are the needs of my children?
- Can I work only the hours that my children are

gone, so that I am always there when they are home?

- Is this their need, or is it my need?
- Does my husband support the decision, and is he willing and able to help out with the children and household responsibilities?

Once you have made your choice to work or stay home full-time, if you still question yourself, check it out. Is it out of traditional belief? Is it out of guilt of what your husband has said? Is it out of the guilt of things that you have read?

If you stay home out of guilt, you will be angry with your children and you will discipline them improperly because you are frustrated. You will feel taken advantage of. "My husband doesn't appreciate me." Those negative emotions will come out of you because you are not doing what is in your heart. You are doing it out of guilt.

A guilty mom does not take the time to think, she *reacts* out of *guilty emotion*. A God-centered mom, however, who is training up her children in the way that they should go, is one who is leading her children in righteousness, and one who considers justice, before acting.

In choosing to be a mom who works outside the home you need to have a plan so you don't say to yourself, "Oh, no, my child is doing this and I should be there." When you act out of guilt, you train your children the wrong way. You give them gifts when you shouldn't. You don't discipline them at times when you should. You allow negative behavior and make excuses for them based on your own guilt and bad feelings. We can't live in a place of guilt all the time.

Know what God has called you to do.

Know what God has called you to do and then do it with all of your heart. Learn how to balance your life, and don't live in guilt. A guilty mom is a dangerous mom. If you feel guilty about areas of your life, then you are constantly living in negativity because guilt does not produce positive emotions.

If you and your husband are in agreement with the child-training choices you have made, then do not let your children place guilt upon you. Kids can be brilliant at times in making their parents feel guilty. My kids have done it: "Well, Mom, you weren't here."

I talk to my kids honestly. I'll say, "You know that you are the priority. You know the value that Dad and I put upon your lives. You know that we consider you the greatest gift God has given to us, and the greatest privilege is raising you to love God and to be healthy and strong for Him on this earth, right?"

Too many of our children are raised with the selfish belief, "I should have this and that; you should get me this; I deserve that." I want to say, "Wait a minute, Sweetheart. You know what? We are here to serve people. That's what we do. People are not here to serve us. Now, is there something that you need?"

Re-examine your life.

Many women never deal with the big picture of guilt. They keep doing what they are doing and keep saying, "I feel so bad." If you feel bad, do something about it. I do not let my children repeat things that are not truth, because if I do, they will begin to believe the words that they say. So if they say words like, "You don't love me," I'll say, "Whoa! We don't talk like that. I do love you." First I reaffirm them and then I set the record straight. Don't get mad at your kids if they say, "You don't love me. You don't care about me. You don't understand me." They are giving you a sign of something going on in their heart, so pay attention.

Once you make the right choice for yourself to work or not to work outside the home, you will feel good about it and you will be sailing high. Don't allow anyone to make you feel guilty. Your kids will know when you feel guilty. But when you take the time to conquer those feelings, you can raise your children without guilt or condemnation.

Take the time to solidify your thoughts, make sure your decision is based on your true desires, prayerfully ask God to guide you, and then get in agreement with your mate.

Questions to Ponder

1. If you are a stay-at-home mom, take a moment to write down your top three reasons for making your choice to stay home full-time with your children.

2. If you are a working mom, take a moment to write down your top three reasons for making the choice to work outside the home.

3. Whichever decision you have made for yourself, do you deal with guilt over your choice? If so, go back over the *questions for determining the route for you* to see if there is an area you can work on.

Chapter 18
Divorce, Single-Parenting, and the Importance of Grandparents in Our Lives

If you live in guilt, it will stifle your spiritual growth and keep you from becoming the kind of person who could really love, minister to, and build up your children.

First, let me say this: Divorce is not the unpardonable sin. One of the number one questions we, as pastors, are asked is about divorce in the church. Anyone who has been through a divorce recognizes that divorce is ugly. But, it is not unforgivable. It doesn't make you a bad person or less of a Christian than a person who has never been divorced.

We have to realize that no one stands before the preacher or the justice of the peace to get married and thinks, "I will get married to this one for a year or two, and then I will get a divorce." No one makes a plan to go through the pain of a divorce. People get married because they *believe* it is going to work, but through bad situations and bad choices, a divorce often results.

There are consequences of divorce.

We have to acknowledge one of the huge challenges in society today is the multiple marriages and divorces many men and women have been through. Although every divorced man and woman suffers to some extent, the ones who suffer the most are always the children caught in the middle of two parents. Too many children live with only one parent.

If you have been divorced, we realize it's a sad situation, but we believe in you as a person and we believe you can be redeemed from what you did in your past. You can be forgiven and walk away from the pain, hurt, and failure. You can have a life of health, success, and prosperity.

I think the hardest part of moving on emotionally from the hurt of a divorce is acknowledging your part and asking for God to forgive you and help cleanse you from your part of the failure. Many people want to put all the blame on the other person and not admit they had any part of it. It could be true that your mate was a dirty dog, and caused most of the problems that led to your divorce. But, what part did you play? It may be very small, but you can ask God to forgive you for that small part.

I think many times men have the hardest time with guilt over a divorce. Because they may not live with their children, they may be dominated by guilt. They may think, *I'm not good enough. I have made horrible mistakes in my life. What can I do?* We cannot relive our past and make it right, but we can say, "Wait a minute. I'm going to start today and be the man that God wants me to be. I will be the person God can look at and say, 'He will command his children after me from this day forward.'"

If you live in guilt, it will stifle your spiritual growth and keep you from becoming the kind of person who could really love, minister to, and build up your children. Guilt will bind you; it will tie you up in knots.

The good news is that you can be free from guilt. You can be free by exchanging it with forgiveness. Go to God and talk with Him about the issues that brought you to the place of failure. Be brutally honest with Him. As I mentioned before, when you go to God, don't try to percentage out your portion of the wrong. And don't percentage out forgiveness. Just go ahead and take it all.

Just say, "God, I am guilty of failure in my marriage." So maybe your mate was 98 percent guilty. That still gives you two percent. You were guilty of some part because you were in a partnership and it failed. Go to God and say, "I can't figure it all out. All I'm saying is, I failed. Please forgive me. Now that you have forgiven me, help me to forgive myself for the failure."

When we have children that are grown, many times

we look at their lives and think of ourselves as failures. Go to God and say, "I have failed as a parent. I look at my children and I see what I put within them. I see the anger, the discouragement, the doubt, and the low self-esteem. I see what's happening in my child's life and I am very sad about it. Father, please forgive me and help me forgive myself. Let me become a new person. Let me walk in a different role. Let me live as a person of compassion, love, and goodness because you have had mercy on me. Now, I'm going to give mercy everywhere I go." That's how to walk in wholeness.

Single-parents:

Many single moms struggle with the feeling that they don't have what it takes to raise their children. I think this is especially true of moms with sons. They feel there is something missing in what they can give to their sons, but God says He is the father to the fatherless.

The best thing you can do is get involved in your local church and become a part of the community of believers. Many churches have smaller groups, single-parent meetings, and support offered in a variety of ways. God has not called you to make it on your own. He will provide for the unique and special needs of your household as you reach out and allow people into your life.

When you can, get family members or other strong people to be surrogate grandparents, aunts, and uncles. Don't think that you alone can meet every need and provide all the support your child needs.

God has all you need to raise your children to be whatever He has called them to be. I want to encourage you to realize you are not alone. You are not taking on the job by yourself. Besides the great people in your life, as you allow

Him into your life, you also have the Comforter, the Provider, and He is well able to make all grace abound towards you!

Biblical examples of parenting (Esther, Moses, and David):

I thought it would be great to explore some examples of the "less than ideal" families from the Bible to see what we can learn. A few examples of parenting by someone other than the biological parents are from Esther and Moses, and we have an example of a dysfunctional family with David.

In the book of Esther, we find that Esther was raised by an uncle after the death of her parents. What a wonderful woman she was. At the appointed time she saved a whole generation of people. She loved God and was a woman of great character. She also had a great relationship with her uncle. She depended upon him and looked to him for prayer and the answers she needed.

Esther did not let the limitations of losing her parents and going to live with her uncle leave her dysfunctional and weak. She certainly didn't have a mom to train her how to take care of herself or how to act in certain situations. But that didn't stop her. She was a lovely woman – inside and out. She obviously loved God and followed after His ways. She was led into the highest place in the land to save her people. God gave her a voice to save a race and change a nation for Him, because she wasn't limited by what she didn't have. She used what she did have for Him.

Moses was given away by his mother in order to preserve his life. She placed him in the safest area she could find, knowing Pharaoh's daughter would rescue him and raise him. Then Pharaoh's daughter hired "a woman" to help with his care. That woman just happened to be Moses' biological mother. This was such a unique situation, used by God to again save the Jewish race.

David was raised in a family of eight children, and he wasn't wanted by his brothers. God told the prophet Samuel, "One of the sons of Jesse will be the next king." So Samuel said to Jesse, "Go get me your sons." Jesse lined up seven of his sons who stood before the prophet. The prophet said, "No, do you have another one?" because he knew this was the place where he was supposed to find the king. None of the seven in Jesse's lineup qualified. Jesse said, "Well, I've got one more. He's out in the field." David's older brothers probably said, "Him? Are you kidding?" Samuel said, "Call him in." David came in and Samuel said, "He's the one. He is to be the next king of Israel."

There are all different kinds of challenging situations in which people are raised, yet they become strong people for God. David was raised in a home where he was not wanted, but still he was raised up strong for God. Esther lost all of her immediate family, yet she saved her nation. Moses had to leave the family in which he was birthed to become part of another family. God recognizes that families have all different kinds of situations. He is not limited by our limitations. He sees the destiny plan for our lives and uses many people and situations to bring His perfect will to pass.
Step-parenting:

I have a close friend who didn't marry until she was in her early thirties. Her husband was a little older than she was, and he had been married previously. When they married she not only became a wife for the first time, she also became the step-mom to a grown daughter and a twelve-year-old daughter. Not an easy task. I spent some time talking with my friend and found she had some really great wisdom to pass along to those who may find themselves in a similar situation:

1. Don't try to be Mom.

It wasn't just "love at first sight" when my friend met her new step-daughters. As a matter of fact, one of them loved and respected her right away, but the other had some major adjustments to make. Because the younger daughter felt like she was betraying her own mom if she let her new step-mom into her life, she slammed the door shut instead.

One of the keys she shared with me was that she didn't try to be *Mom* to her new step-daughter. In fact, she sat down with her and told her she wasn't trying to take her mom's place and never would. Her new daughter was so guarded and closed to the new relationship it took many years to produce a healthy, great relationship.

2. Sow into the relationship.

The next thing she did was sow into the relationship. She knew that if she wanted to have a great relationship with her new step-daughter she would have to sow the seeds into her heart. She poured herself into sowing kind acts and words. She would say to her, "I love you," without expecting anything in return. She would tell her, "I thank God for bringing you into my life."

When you can hug or touch, do so. Ask questions about their day and really listen. Help out with homework or other projects when you can. There are many ways you can sow into the relationship when you are creative and seeking ways to give. If you want a good relationship to develop, you will have to pour into it first.

3. Communicate the roles in your household.

It may seem simple, but another great key to successful blending of families is to communicate clearly the roles of everyone in the home. The father in this situation sat everyone down and said to his daughter, "I love you very much, and as my daughter, I will always love you. One day you will grow up and leave home, but my wife will be with me forever. Her role in my life is very, very important. She is not going to take the place of your mother, but she is an authority figure in your life and you will treat her with respect."

The children need to recognize their role and the role of the adults in the house. Many children will try to play on the emotions and feelings of guilt. They will generally try to manipulate their parents into getting their own way. You have to be strong in knowing and communicating the boundaries and roles of authority.

4. Don't talk bad about their other parent.

Not talking bad about the other parent is so vital to having the healthy, godly relationships you desire in a blended family. It is possible that the absent parent has made bad decisions and is living out the negative consequences of their choices. The other parent may be on drugs, sleeping around, partying all night long, and can't keep a job, but what are *you* going to do? If you are wise, you will keep your hand over your mouth. Wisdom is not allowing yourself to speak badly of your ex-wife or ex-husband, or your mate's ex-spouse.

Kids are smart. They don't need you to tell them what is right and what is wrong, especially when it is right in front of them. The best thing to do is live the lifestyle you want them to emulate – and that includes keeping our mouths in line with the Word of God.

I'm not saying to ignore unsafe situations or allow your children to stay where they are in danger. I am saying you need to stay positive and speak whatever encouraging words you can. If there is something negative going on, do your best to speak kindly and offer to pray with your child for their parent. Try to put yourself in the other person's place. Do for them what you would want done for you. Say those things about them that you would want said about you. Remember, you are sowing good seed into the hearts of your children.

The importance of grandparents in our lives.

Sadly, in our world today many grandparents do not understand the importance of their role or take it seriously. They don't see the value of the role God has given to them on this earth to love, train, teach, and feed health into their grandchildren.

I wasn't raised around my grandparents, but I had "adoptive" grandparents all the time because I was raised in church. In every church my dad pastored, there were always grandparents who "adopted" all of us Peterson kids. They wanted to impart into our lives and would feed life and goodness into us. They would take the role of grandparents and did all the special things grandparents do.

Casey was very strongly influenced by his mom's dad. Casey really looked to his grandfather as a father figure in his life. His grandfather's own children would tell you he had some rip-roaring problems and he wasn't a great father, but he was a wonderful grandfather to my husband. (I never got to meet Casey's grandfather because he died when Casey was in his later teenage years.)

Casey's grandfather lived down the street from him, and he fed into Casey's life. His grandfather was an alcoholic, but he didn't let Casey see that part of him. They were not a church-going family, but his grandfather would always say to Casey, "You are my number one grandson. You are smart. You are going to do great things in life." He encouraged Casey with his words, and he built him up with love and positive words.

If your children are grown and you are looking at your lack of success as a parent, I want to encourage you to jump in the race again because of what you can do for your grandchildren. You can feed into the lives of your grandchildren.

I would have to say that Casey's grandfather more significantly set the course of Casey's life than did his own father. His grandfather spoke life into Casey and believed in him. He didn't do it with his own children, but he did do it with Casey. So, grandparents rise up and recognize, "I can set the course of life for my grandchildren."

I think it is very sad to see the older people in the church who don't recognize their value to the young ones coming up. (It is also sad to see young people without respect and honor towards their grandparents and the elderly.) There is so much wisdom and love that is needed everywhere you look. But many times we sit back and feel like we aren't needed or wanted. Take the time to look around and find someone to which you can give of yourself. When you give, it will be given unto you: good measure, pressed down, and shaken together (Luke 6:38a). God will bring great joy and blessing into your life as you give!

Questions to Ponder

1. Have you been divorced in your past? If so, have you gotten free of the guilt over your divorce? If not, take a moment to ask God for forgiveness.

2. If you are a step-parent, write down one key to step-parenting that you can use to better your relationship with your step-child.

3. Think about the influence of "grandparents" in your own life. Take a moment to ponder a favorite memory with your grandparents.

4. Do your children have special "grandparents" in their lives? If not, consider how you can help fill that spot in your children's lives. (Maybe find an older couple in the church and begin to build a relationship with them.)

CONCLUSION

I really do love being a parent! For me it is one of the best parts of God's inheritance to us as His children. What a great joy it has been for Casey and me to raise our own children, and to watch our friends and congregation members raising theirs using these same principles.

As I move to the end of my hands-on parenting years, I look forward to what God has planned for our family in the decades to come as my adult children mature. I adore being a parent to our children, but I have also loved seeing the babies in our church grow into teens and then on to become adults who love God and serve Him faithfully.

When you hold your babies in your arms, it's hard to realize how fast time will fly. It all goes by quicker than you can imagine.

Amidst the challenges involved and the demand on your patience and time, I encourage you to praise God daily for the gift He has brought to you in your children. What a wonderful privilege and blessing it is to be a parent and to raise our children to grow up loving and serving God.

For more teaching materials by Casey and Wendy Treat on
this or other topics, please write to us at:
Casey Treat Ministries
P.O. Box 98800
Seattle, WA 98198
or visit our website at:
www.caseytreat.com

I Love This Thing Called Parenting...